Cycling Through A

Also by Julia R May

My Feet and Other Animals

Walking Pembrokeshire with a Fruitcake

Walking with Offa

Pedals, Panniers and Punctures

Walking with Hadrian

I've Cycled Through There

Cycling Across England

Cycles and Sandcastles

A Week in Provence

Bicycles, Boats and Bagpipes

Bicycles, Beer and Black Forest Gateau

Dawdling Through The Dales

Dedication.

For my mother, Rose May. She is the last person to remember them.

Prologue

In an overheated room in a sheltered housing complex in Burnley there is a small, carved wooden box. The box is a depository for memories, half remembered or forgotten entirely. Inside this box are two life times of old photographs, some sepia, some black and white, known and unknown ancestors; and laid carefully on top of them all sits a newspaper clipping, faded and torn at the edges, over one hundred years old now, pasted to an old piece of card.

The clipping was taken from the Burnley Express which in 1916 was running a regular feature of Burnley families and the contributions they were making to the war effort. Together with a brief statement the clipping shows eight head and shoulder, passport-style photographs of mother and father, Maria and Thomas Ruddeforth and six of their sons. One son is in a reserved occupation, one son is too young to fight but is working in a local munitions factory. The other four sons are in uniform, serving soldiers in the Great War, two of them are in the Accrington Pals.

The occupant of this hot, stuffy little room and keeper of this box of memories is a lady in her late eighties, frail now and suffering from Alzheimer's Disease, her memory is fading like the contents of the box. She is my mother, Rose. The youngest son in the old newspaper clipping is her father, my grandfather, Herbert Ruddeforth.

There is another photograph that I found when emptying my mum's house following her move into sheltered housing. Too large to fit in the wooden box, it had been resting on some old documents in a desk. It is now framed and sits on a shelf in my own home, and sitting next to it is a framed studio portrait of my mum as a toddler. This larger photograph is another studio portrait, one of thousands that were produced at the time of the Great War. It depicts my mum's uncle by marriage, William Whalley, looking serious and proud in his army uniform.

My paternal grandfather, Frank May, born in the last years of the old century, would have been old enough to enlist towards the end of the war.

My partner, Mike, also had a relative who served in the Great War. His father's older cousin, John Withers, had left his farming life in Westmorland and enlisted in the Gordon Highlanders where he served as Private.

The politics, the tactics, the hard fought battles and the history of the First World War are complicated and this is not intended to be a history book. Instead it is an account of two people's cycle ride along the northern end of the Western Front. Mike and I set out deliberately in 2018, one hundred years since the end of the first mechanised war in history, to cycle just a small section of the Front; with only a week to spare we did not want to hurry along the Western Front, cycling it all but seeing little, instead we chose to concentrate on the northern section of the Front – Flanders and The Somme – thus allowing enough time to see all we wished to in that area. We wanted to trace our own ancestors' routes through the fields of Flanders and Picardy, to see for ourselves this small corner of the globe that had witnessed so much, and to learn more about a generation, now all dead, that had gladly marched into battle believing the sacrifice they were making would make the world a better place.

It was expected to be over by Christmas, the conflict that was to become known as the war to end all wars. The Great War. It started with a single shot in a town in Eastern Europe, a town that few in Britain had even heard of, with the murder of an Archduke that equally few were aware even existed. The murderer, Gavrilo Princip not only condemned himself to death but millions of other Europeans and Commonwealth citizens too. Germany committed itself to supporting Austria-Hungary in their reprisals against the Serbs. It could and should have ended there but Kaiser Wilhelm had ambitions for Imperial Germany, he wanted a superpower to not only rival but surpass Great Britain. He thought his task was God given, believed it was written in the Bible, and was determined to succeed. And so the inter-married royal houses of Europe went to war. In the words of Harry Patch, who died in 2009 having been the last survivor of the First World War: 'T'isn't worth it... if you boil it down, what was it? Nothing but a family row. That's what caused it. T'isn't worth it.'

In the ensuing complicated political turmoil of summer 1914 Germany marched into neutral Belgium, and honouring the 1839 Treaty of London that guaranteed Belgium independence and neutrality, Britain responded by declaring war on Germany on 4th August. The German army was aiming to capture Paris and take France out of the war before turning their attention to Russia. By 5th September the Germans were a mere ten miles from Paris but the Allies of Belgian, France and Britain brought their advance to a halt: this was the First Battle of the Marne. So desperate were the Allies to halt the advance that Paris taxis were used to move 4000 French troops to the front. The Germans retreated, chased by the Allies, until the Belgian coast was reached.

Both sides faced one another, no one was giving ground and by October trenches were being dug. This line of trenches was to become known as the Western Front and would soon extend from the North Sea coast at Nieuwpoort in Belgium all the way to the Franco Swiss border at Pfetterhouse, a distance of 460 miles. In Belgium the natural features of the landscape dictated where the Western Front was established: in the northern part of Belgium the River Yser with its deltas, reaches and flood plains, to the south were the hills making up ridges on which, the soon to be infamous, villages of Messines and Passchendaele sat. The old centuries' wars of move and counter-move had turned into a war of attrition and stalemate fought across a narrow strip of land running for hundreds of miles through Belgium and France. Lives would be sacrificed on both sides for the next four years as ground was fought over, lost, regained and lost again.

Pre-war, the Germany Army was a well-trained fighting force with a reserve of over 4 million trained men. The German equivalent of National Service ensured that all men between the ages of 17 and 45 were eligible to serve. In comparison the British Army consisted of a small professional force of 247,000 soldiers; these were further supported by Territorials and Reserves, making a combined number of just over 700,000 men. When war was declared almost 200,000 British men enlisted in the first five months. Many did so with patriotic pride and for some of the poorer in society the war presented them with the chance of excitement, regular meals, decent pay and an escape from the drudge and poverty of everyday life. But these recruits were not the battle-hardened experienced soldiers needed to fight against the German might and the British Army found itself at a distinct disadvantage. Lord Kitchener was hastily made Secretary of State for War; unlike many in power at the time he expect the war to last for several years and, foreseeing a need for a rapidly expanding army, he set about creating his Pals Battalions in an effort to increase recruitment. Men from factories, football clubs and towns enlisted together. With the outbreak of war the stock markets around the world went into turmoil. One thousand six hundred workers of the London Stock Exchange volunteered, forming the Stock Exchange Battalion of the Royal Fusiliers - another Pals Battalion - it was one of the first to be raised in August 1914. Four hundred of them never came home.

With the men off fighting the war, women suddenly found themselves taking on additional roles. Many took over the jobs the men had been doing, many found new forms of work directly involved in the war effort in munitions factories. By 1916 branches of the armed forces were beginning to be established specifically for women, and by the end of the war over 100,000 women were serving in the military in non-combatant jobs as drivers, nurses, cooks, mechanics, clerks and in other vital roles. The Commonwealth War Graves Commission only officially recognises 655 women as war deaths. But many more were killed in the factories, died of disease whilst serving behind the front line or died of other causes whilst serving. An estimated 1500 women died in the First World War. Many nurses died on the Western Front when advanced field dressing stations and casualty clearing stations they were working in were bombed. Many other nurses died when hospital ships they were on were sunk.

Of course the Western Front was not the only theatre of war in the First World War. Other parts of the globe became enmeshed in the conflict with fighting taking place in Turkey, on the mountains of the Italian Alps, in the Balkans, Russia, Egypt, East Africa, parts of the Middle East and other places. But for Britain in particular it is the Western Front where most of our fighting forces were concentrated and with its close proximity to Britain it is the place most easily reached. So it is probably inevitable that it is the Western Front that has been most keenly remembered and immortalised by film, books and television, and by authors, artists and poets of that time.

Saturday 26th May 2018

In the late afternoon we left our van in Hull and boarded the ferry for an overnight crossing to Zeebrugge. With our bikes safely stowed in the hold along with about a dozen other cycles and various cars, caravans, campervans and motorbikes, we made our way to the upper deck to watch the ship sail down the River Humber to the North Sea. Once the ship hit the open water we made our way inside to the lounge.

"This ship's remarkably stable," commented Mike just as I staggered sideways into a wall.

"You think?"

Before going to bed that evening we made sure our phones and my watch were set to European time: forward an hour. A school boy error had sent us into a panic on another ferry crossing at the end of a previous cycling holiday and I did not relish another mistake like that one. But we were awoken in the early hours not by my alarm but by a message from my network provider.

"What was that?" muttered Mike sleepily from the bunk above.

"It says," I read, "'Welcome to the USA, rates for using your mobile abroad can be found at the following web address.' Why on earth does it think we're in the States?"

"Maybe we turned right instead of left," Mike replied.

"We have got on the right ship haven't we?" I muttered sarcastically.

The only response was a snore.

Sunday 27th May 2018. 57 miles.

By the morning my mobile provider had decided we were indeed in Belgium, although costs of calling home were no less extortionate than calling from the USA. The ferry docked on time and we cycled off the ferry and were quickly through passport control and heading for the sea front amongst a peloton of British and Belgian cyclists. It was handy to follow the local cyclists who knew just where they were heading to leave the busy port. Immediately we were on Belgian soil and we were on a cycle route, designated, marked out in red tarmac and separated from the busy road. We were to find this would be the case for most of our cycling through this little country where cyclists were well catered for on all the roads and given priority over cars at junctions and roundabouts. But where Belgian authorities had been kind to cyclists the weather had been less kind and a mini sand dune had blown onto the cycle route before we even left the dock area. The Belgians cycled through the sand undaunted but the British cyclists all got off and carried their bikes.

"I've just cleaned my bike," remarked one young woman, staggering under the weight of four panniers as she heaved her bike over the sand.

Soon we reached the promenade and cycled swiftly along, but barely two miles into our ride we reached a dead end and had to turn round and leave the promenade along a side road.

"That's good going for us," laughed Mike. "A full two miles before we've got lost."

We were hugging the coast, heading for Nieuwpoort, which at the start of the First World War had marked the northern end of the Western Front. The coast road was busy with traffic but the cycle route ran along the pavement sparing us the multitude of vehicles on that busy Sunday morning. The cycle route consisted for most of the way of large block paving, which was for the most part smooth and comfortable to ride over but at times had a camber to rival the Manchester Velodrome. Bright red poppies grew at the side of the path and the dunes rose on our right, covered with marram grass. It was a pleasant ride on that hot sunny morning. We passed through several seaside towns, where cars and trams shared the road to our left. The smell of chips and hot waffles taunted us as we cycled along. Locals were out on their own bikes and we kept passing and being passed by a young English couple who had cycled off the ferry with us.

Ten days before our holiday I had been cycling to work as usual. It had been a beautiful spring morning so I had taken the long way, the scenic, calorie-burning circular tour of Pendle Hill. It was twenty two miles to work, careful miles as I had a cake tin full of chocolate beetroot muffins bungeed to the pannier rack. I carefully avoided the pot holes, the bumpy patches of tarmac, the two harsh cattle grids and arrived at a junction close to work with the muffins safely intact. And then I did something stupid. Nothing unusual there, I do lots of stupid things. But this was a first. I stopped and put my left foot to the ground, and then I leaned to the right! In slow motion I teetered on the edge of balance. The muffins! And then I fell sideways, still with my right foot firmly in the toe clip of the pedal. My right thigh, knee and both hands banged onto the tarmac, the pedal gouged into my left shin and my right ankle twisted in the clip. My first thought, after the muffins, was has anyone seen me? No. Thank goodness. The slight ache in my right ankle was out-throbbed by my stinging knee and palms and my aching thigh. It was only after a shower at work and a cup of tea and a partially disassembled muffin that I became aware that whilst other bits had stopped hurting my ankle was beginning to ramp up the pain. Elevation, ice and painkillers seemed to do the trick and I cycled home, ignoring my own advice as a first aider to rest a sprain. That was a mistake and later that evening I could hardly bare to put any weight on my foot. Three hours spent in Urgent Care and several X-rays later ruled out a fracture but my ankle was badly sprained. I spent the following two days off work and the weekend recuperating, meanwhile my colleagues sent me texts, emails and messages of the 'delicious muffins, shame they're a bit bashed up' and 'only you could manage to fall off a stationary bike' variety. The silly fall could have been a lot worse but for a few days it looked as if the cycling holiday would have to be cancelled. As the swelling went down, the bruising came up and my foot began to resemble the colour of the muffins. For once I was a good patient, determined to be recovered in time for our cycling holiday.

"Those toe clips are coming off," Mike had asserted and I readily agreed. The last thing I wanted was to risk further injury that would jeopardise our holiday.

So as we cycled along the coast that morning I was hoping my ankle would continue to hold up. But falling off was the last thing on my mind. After about an hour of riding we seemed to be making good progress and we had reached the small town of De Haan. The cycle path was leading us through a more suburban area slightly inland and now instead of dunes with marram grass and poppies we had a pine wood on our right. The large grey block paving had been replaced by smaller red block paving on a dual use path that cyclists shared with pedestrians. On a sweeping bend with no one in sight and Mike half a dozen yards ahead of me I was contemplating social media of all things when I misjudged the bend and the rear wheel dropped off the edge of the block paving into the sandy soil. The bike flipped to the left instantly. There was no time to even try to save myself and I crashed into the block paving with hands and feet still on the bike. My left arm and elbow gouged across two edges of block paving, leaving two strips of missing skin that ran half the length of my forearm, and the front of my left shoulder slammed into the ground. The pain was agonising and I lay there, still on the bike and clutching my left shoulder.

Mike had heard the crash and I could hear him rushing back and asking if I was okay. He feared I had dislocated my shoulder. I knew I hadn't done that and I managed to sit up, still clutching my shoulder, feeling nauseous and shaking and sweating profusely. Belgians seemed to appear from every direction offering assistance and phone numbers for doctors, non-emergency numbers, emergency numbers, ambulance and directions to the nearest hospital. Aware that I was sitting firmly in the middle of the cycle path I got unsteadily to my feet and went and sat at the side of the path, removing my helmet and glasses and mopping my face with a handkerchief.

"Is it dislocated?" Mike asked.

"No, but I think I've done something serious and I feel sick."

"Have a drink," he said, passing me the water bottle.

"Can you move it?" he asked, reaching out a tentative hand to touch my shoulder.

"Don't touch it!" I growled and he quickly withdrew his hand.

More people were gathering offering help and showing a touching amount of concern. It's always embarrassing when you trip up or fall over and falling off a bike is no exception. I didn't want a fuss or an audience and managed to reassure people I was okay. As the crowds moved away we began to assess my injuries. A severely grazed left arm and elbow, a shoulder that was hammering out pain far worse than when I broke my wrist, a red graze where my left knee cap used to be, a couple of scratches on my right knee and a graze on my left little finger and the back of my left hand. Later bruising would also appear on my left hip and even a couple of scratches on my back. And the left drop of my handlebars was a lot nearer to the right than it used to be.

"Oh, my bike!"

"It's okay, it will knock back," Mike reassured, giving the side of the handlebars a few hard whacks until it was realigned. "Now, how's that shoulder?"

"I'm okay," I gasped.

"Are you okay to continue?"

Was I? We had planned this holiday months ago, the accommodation was booked, research had been done and if I could not get back on that bike and ride the holiday would be over. I stood up, put my helmet back on, not easy one handed, and swung my leg over the bike. I could barely stretch my left arm out to reach the handlebars, the pain was excruciating. As for stretching it far enough to be able to change gear, that was impossible. I climbed back off.

"I'm in the wrong gear, you'll have to change down onto the middle chain ring for me," I said.

Mike gave me a look that questioned if I really was fit to continue but changed gear and then held the bike as I climbed back on. We set off with me in front that time to set the pace. Slow. I cycled for the rest of the day without using my left hand except to brake, fortunately I had cross top brakes fitted to the top of the bars when

I first got the bike so at least I was able to reach the lever. As for gear changing that was all done by my right hand for the next three days. For much of the time I just held my left arm across my body, stretching it out was too painful. I was fearful I had broken something, either my collar bone or the top of the bone in my upper arm but I was determined not to say anything. Every movement of my arm resulted in an odd crunching popping sensation in the top of my shoulder. I decided that if it had bruised and swollen by the evening then I would have to find a hospital and get it checked out. If I could ride for the rest of the day then hopefully I would be okay to continue after that.

When I later posted pictures of the grazes on social media all my friends immediately told me to get it checked out. As a first aider it's the advice I would give to anyone but as one friend said, first aiders never take their own advice. By the end of the day there was no bruising and just a little swelling. Mike's sister, a nurse, thought it likely I had torn a ligament. Dosed up on ibuprofen I was able to cycle with increasing ease of movement as the days passed but for the rest of that day I was very nervous of going fast and of falling off again.

The English cyclists must have stopped somewhere, they passed us again about half an hour after my crash. Finding ourselves lined up alongside one another at a set of traffic lights in a pleasant town they asked where we were heading.

"Ypres today," replied Mike.

"Oh, same as us."

"Just don't do the same as me," I commented, indicating my left arm.

"Have you got a first aid kit?" asked the woman, wincing in sympathy.

We reached Ostend, passing the docks, railway and a busy marina. Roads were coming at us from all directions but the Belgian cycle paths were well signed and easy to follow and soon our route returned us to the coast road. The sandy beach on our right was busy with people sunbathing and swimming. We were cycling along a broad promenade once more, there were tram tracks on our left and then the main coast road and beyond that sand dunes dotted with concrete bunkers and gun emplacements left over from the Second World War. Although our cycle ride was all about the First World War we were often to come across reminders of both World Wars during our trip, this region of Europe had seen more than its share of invading armies in the twentieth century.

We stopped to take a photo of the bunkers before applying sun screen to our arms, legs and faces. I had propped my bike against the chain barrier separating the promenade from the tram tracks when an approaching tram sounded its horn.

"Go on," laughed Mike. "Get your bike snatched up by a passing tram and run over."

"It's not on the tram tracks," I replied before nevertheless checking the bike was in no danger.

We reached Nieuwpoort and stopped for lunch, finding a shady bench near the King Albert I Monument. It was the first of many memorials we would come across commemorating the First World War. The circular monument was fronted by neat cobbles, with a war memorial guarded by stone lions and surrounded by a network of roads.

From Nieuwpoort we turned inland, heading south towards Ypres. Our plan was to follow the cycle route on what had been an old First World War tramway but the bridge accessing the cycle route had collapsed and we had to retrace our route back and then across the River Yser and along a road before we could rejoin the old tramway further south. We followed this gravelled cycle way for some miles to Diksmuide, passing various concrete ruins, all that were left of old bunkers from the war.

The cycle route crossed the river at Diksmuide but before we even reached the cross roads we had been able to see two tall structures to the right of the main road. One was the PAX gate, a stone tower with an arch through the middle. It had been constructed in 1950 using stones from the ruined Ijzer Tower that had been blown up in protest against the Flemish Independence Movement in 1928. Behind and through the PAX gate was a green sward leading to the new Ijzer Tower, at 84 metres in height it was difficult to miss, and is a monument to peace. Equally difficult to miss was a temporary art installation entitled 'Floating Dreams, Art at Peace' consisting of white silhouettes of figures on the sides of the tower and more white life-sized figures of children dotted about the grass surrounding the tower. It was all a bit Anthony Gormley meets a village cricket match. The whole area was surrounded by wire fencing, neat low hedges and in one corner wire gabions filled with rusting shell casings.

Just after leaving Diksmuide, following a quiet lane close to the river, we saw the young British couple coming slowly towards us. The woman was cycling whilst her partner pushed his bike.

"Puncture!" he exclaimed by way of explanation.

"Our spare inner tube has a Shraeder valve and it won't fit through the hole in the wheel rim," explained his girlfriend. "Do you have Presta valves? Are your tyres the same width as ours?"

They were not. Our road bikes have skinnier racing tyres, this couple were on hybrid touring bikes with wider tyres.

"Oh well, we'll have to stay at Diksmuide tonight and get a new tube in the morning when the shops open," sighed the woman.

It was an easy but frustrating mistake to make, buying an inner tube with the wrong type of valve. A mistake that had now cost this couple a day's travelling. But why, I wondered could they not patch the puncture? They wished us safe journey and continued back to town, we didn't see them again.

Our route continued along quiet minor roads lined with large fields of wheat and barley. In the field margins wildflowers grew thick and colourful. The poppies were ever present but there were also the delicate blue of cornflowers and yellow and white camomile. Fat muscular cows grazed in some fields, and not just that afternoon but on other days we were frequently cycling with the scent of pig muck in the air. Essence de porcine seemed to be a feature of the ride.

It had been a humid and sultry afternoon. The clear sunny skies of the morning having been replaced by build ups of increasingly grey cloud. Cycling along and creating a breeze helped to cool us but each time we stopped we were quickly bathed in sweat that the still air did little to evaporate. Thunder clouds seemed to chase us south for most of the afternoon, never quite catching us, and we reached the outskirts of Ypres and our first B&B at 5.30 p.m. without getting caught in a storm.

Storing the bikes in the garage we were shown to our ground floor room by the middle aged owner. We were much in need of a shower and a cup of tea but I could barely raise my arm and Mike had to assist me not just in getting undressed but in hair washing, combing and putting it into a pony tail.

"You didn't dress the kids very often, did you?" I asked as he battled to get my arms into a T-shirt.

"Yes I did, but they weren't as accident prone as you! And I did their hair. I even tried plaits once or twice."

"I'm impressed but I'll settle for a ponytail thanks."

Dressed and with hair in an interesting arrangement we set off to walk into Ypres for something to eat. Shortly after leaving the house we had already passed two First World War cemeteries, one on either side of the road. It seemed odd to see them in the middle of a residential street, with houses, garages and gardens surrounding them, but at the time these two small cemeteries were consecrated there would have been no modern estate of houses on this quiet road.

We soon reached the centre of this ancient town to find it was busy with traffic, locals and tourists. People strolled in the square and sat at tables outside bustling cafes, bars and restaurants, many of the shops were still open and we quickly found a small convenience store from which we could buy something to eat, preferring a picnic tea rather than the expensive and crowded eating establishments. We were quickly learning Belgium could be expensive if you were travelling on a budget. We were able to find an empty seat in the large square by the Cloth Hall where we shared a baguette, some Bruges cheese, tomatoes, bananas and custard filled donuts. We watched as a women's choir, all dressed in smart black dresses, each wearing a poppy, assembled and began to walk towards Menin Gate.

At the outbreak of the Great War, Ypres, as the city was known at the time, was a prosperous and beautiful place. Ypres is the French name, today the Flemish name of Ieper is used but few outside of Belgium will recognise it by that name. The British Tommys called it Wipers, easier to pronounce for one thing and with typical squaddie humour. The British soldiers changed many of the French place names they were stationed nearby to easier to pronounce English names. Auchonvillers became Ocean Villas, Mouquet Farm near Pozieres became Moo Cow Farm, the town of Ploegsteert was referred to as Plugstreet and the Tommies much preferred their name of Gerty Wears Velvet instead of the vowel-rich Goedesversvelde.

Ypres has been recorded as early as 1066 and has long been an important town sitting as it does on a trading route to the coast between England, France and The Netherlands. Since the Middle Ages, when Ypres was under French control, it has been a prosperous cloth town, building links with the English wool trade and producing its own lace, woollens and other fabrics. As with many old towns and cities Ypres was quite heavily fortified in the past; in the late fourteenth century it had no fewer than nine gates set into its city walls. Throughout history the area surrounding Ypres has been the scene of many wars as various rulers of France and its provinces as well as the English, Spanish, Dutch and Austro Hungarians have scuffled over the region and its religion. Ypres has been under siege and attacked on numerous occasions down the centuries, but all this was as nothing compared to the total destruction wrought during the First World War.

In 1914 Ypres was still a wealthy town dependant on trades of cloth and materials of all kinds and their associated industries such as dyes and tanning, as well as lace and soap making. And it was still an important trading post with numerous canals and railways. It even had its own garrison. Ironically from 1895 up to the outbreak of the Great War there had been a large restoration project underway at Ypres with the aim of preserving and renovating many of the city's historic buildings. They just finished in time to see them all flattened. With its canal and rail network Ypres was seen as a strategically important place by both sides during the War and was heavily fought over for the duration of the conflict. The Ypres Salient, a curving bulge, formed the front line around the town but four years of bombardments ensured the German Army never actually occupied the town, not that there was anything left standing to physically occupy.

After the war the medieval centre was faithfully rebuilt. One of the most notable buildings, Lakenhalle, occupies a central location in the old part of the city and dominates the skyline with its 70 metre high belfry. The original Lakenhalle, or Cloth Hall, was finished in 1304 and had been located on the banks of the Ieperslee River from where ships could be unloaded with their cargoes of wool. Today the river has been covered over, a bit like the rivers in Burnley but with less litter. On the first floor of the Lakenhalle the area that had originally been used to store the wool is now the location of the In Flanders Fields Museum. It was not until 1969 that the Staidhuis was rebuilt on the eastern side of Lakenhalle and unlike the rest of the building the Staidhuis is only a partial copy of the 1619 original.

To the east of the medieval centre of Ypres is Menin Gate, located guarding the moat and on the route that the soldiers marching to the front would have taken. Menin Gate is a monument to the missing of the First World War. Missing soldiers of course can have no known grave, they cannot be buried and their final resting place marked with a headstone, their bodies cannot be repatriated. Their loved ones have no grave to visit, nowhere to lay flowers, to pay their respects. It was suggested at the end of the war that the totally obliterated town of Ypres be purchased by Britain and left in ruins as a permanent memorial to the dead. Instead it was finally decided that memorials to the missing would be erected along the Western Front and there are now numerous memorials to the missing with no known graves. Each monument is individually designed but all have several features in common. They usually consist of red brick and pale stone. They each, just like the First World War cemeteries, have a register to help relatives find their loved ones' names. The fallen of each Regiment are listed together along with their rank, surname and initial or first name. Each monument is carved with thousands of names. The main memorials are the Missing of the Somme at Thiepval (72,193 names), Menin Gate Memorial to the Missing at Ypres (54,896 names), Messines Ridge Memorial to the New Zealand war dead (828 names) and the Tyne Cot Memorial to the Missing (34,949 names). These figures are not fixed. Occasionally the remains of soldiers are uncovered either due to archaeology, construction or agricultural activity. If these remains can be identified then they will be buried with full honours in one of the many military cemeteries or repatriated if the families so wish, and their names removed from the list of the missing on whichever memorial they appear. The cemeteries too have walls carved with names of the missing from battles fought nearby. Thousands and thousands with no known grave; and each cemetery, each monument to the missing bears the inscription suggested by Rudyard Kipling, who lost his own son in the Great War, 'Known unto God'.

There are however, men who died during the First World War, on the Western Front and in other theatres of war, that do not have their place amongst the rows of thousands in the cemeteries or their names carved on the monuments to the missing. They are not considered missing and neither, at the time, were they considered to have died for their country. These are the over 300 men who were executed, shot at dawn by a firing squad made up of fellow soldiers, for military offenses such as desertion, casting away of arms and cowardice. Today these men would be diagnosed with post-traumatic stress disorder and could hope to receive some sort of treatment. During the period of the First World War and up to 1930 the death penalty could be served for military offenses that included the three above offenses and also disobedience, striking an officer and quitting or being found asleep at their post. In total during the First World War the British Army conducted 230,000 Courts Martial, not just for these but for other offenses too, some of which might include rape and murder. Over 3000 were given the death sentence, although only (only!) 346 were actually carried out. Of these 346, 40 men had committed crimes that also carried the death sentence in civilian law.

Britain was not alone in executing members of its armed forces in this way, most nations involved in the war did the same, it was seen as a way to set an example. How backward that reasoning seems now. Attitudes change, justice is now seen to be fairer and more compassionate. But why did it take until 2007 before an Act of Parliament granted the 306 servicemen executed for military offences posthumous pardons? I cannot help but feel pardon is perhaps the wrong word. To me it implies they did something wrong. Surely the sentiment the British establishment should be issuing is 'apology'. Finally with the creation of the National Memorial Arboretum in Staffordshire these unjustly executed 306 servicemen have now been commemorated. On so many levels the First World War was a bloody horrible affair.

Each evening at eight o'clock at Menin Gate the Last Post is sounded and the streets leading to the Menin Gate fill with people going to pay their respects to men long since dead, their bodies long since lost on the battlefields of Flanders, reduced to dust in some corner of a foreign field. This daily ceremony first started in 1928; how long will it continue, I wonder.

The design of Menin Gate is similar to other First World War memorials with its towering walls and arches constructed of red brick and white stone. Carved lions sit atop the monument and on the outsides are stone colonnades. When it was inaugurated in 1927 by Field Marshal Plumer, this former First World War commander famously said of the men with no known graves: 'He's not missing, he's here'. It is the closest many relatives would ever come to finding their loved ones.

We joined the crowds at the Menin Gate that evening waiting for this moving ceremony to begin. At a few minutes before 8 p.m. the crowd fell silent as an official asked that no one clap at any point during or at the end of the ceremony. Then even the jackdaws fell silent as the last post was sounded, then a reading was given and the women's choir sang. The only sound to break the minute's silence was a solitary blackbird singing from one of the tall trees close to the gate. A lone piper played a lament on his bagpipes. As the ceremony at Menin Gate ended and people began to drift away we climbed the path up onto the top of the grassy rampart leading to one of the outside walls of the monument. The names of the missing cover nearly every surface of the monument. The East Lancashire Regiment was there, occupying several panels. The Pals Regiments of my own corner of Lancashire had lost hundreds of men on the Ypres Salient alone before they even got to The Somme. Next to them were carved the names of the missing of the East Surrey Regiment. The regiments, the names went on and on.

Monday 28th May 2018. 66 miles

"See you on Friday!" called our host as he waved us off from the B&B that morning.

We had booked to spend another night with him on our route back to the coast on the return leg of our journey. And with a good breakfast inside me that included two good cups of tea I was looking forward to it.

My grazes were beginning to heal but my left shoulder was still virtually immovable, and once again I cycled for much of the day with my arm either resting on the handlebars or across my stomach to ease the pain, made worse by any jolt as the bike went over even the slightest bump in the road. Having posted photos of my impressive looking grazes on social media and to the girls' messenger group at work I had been receiving lots of concerned and even more good-natured teasing comments.

"Be more bloody careful you dozy cow!!!! Xx"

"You plonker, time for a tricycle I think."

"Julia stop it!!"

"Face in hands in despair! Hope you're ok though!!"

"Ouch!"

And the most caring: "That looks sore!"

Ah, you can always rely on friends to remind you what an idiot you are. But their concern was genuine and they even managed to gang up on me on Facebook with a multi user advice session that extended to Mike's sister and even my aunt. All offering lots of good advice along the lines of 'get to a hospital and get it checked out' (which I ignored) and 'don't let it stiffen up' (which I took) and 'it sounds like you've ripped something' which I took as reassurance that at least nothing was broken.

Unfortunately as far as bumpy surfaces go there seemed to be rather a lot on the Belgian cycle paths as many of them were either block paving or slabs of poured concrete, and many of the town centres have cobbled streets. As we cycled over the cobbles of the main square in Ypres that morning, through the much quieter Menin Gate and out along the very road the regiments of soldiers would have marched along towards the Front one hundred years ago, I was just grateful I was still able to continue. Barely beyond the old town walls of Ypres and we came to the first cemetery of the day: Menin Road Cemetery.

We soon left Ypres behind, heading east on quiet country lanes surrounded by fields of asparagus, strawberries, beans and potatoes. 'Te Koop' signs dotted the roadsides, advertising various produce as being 'for sale'. It was a sultry morning, hot and humid and overcast but the forecast was for a sunny afternoon to come. The next Commonwealth War Graves cemetery we came to was locked, with a sign on the gate saying the key code could be obtained from the Tourist Information Centre in Ypres. We moved on, there was, depressingly, any number of other cemeteries to look at.

Our first stop of the morning was at Hill 60, barely a hill at all, but with views across the fields to the towers of Ypres in the misty distance. A monument close to the road marked the Battle and on the other side of the road was a field full of poppies. It could not have been more emblematic. This section of the Ypres Salient was fought over for much of the war and was lost and retaken by both sides several times. The land here was purchased by a family from Britain not long after the war, and the landscape left intact, a very visual reminder of how the war left the land, and one of the few remaining areas of battle that have not been turned back to agricultural land in the decades since the end of the conflict. Apart from a few information boards, some poppy wreaths and the duckboards to protect the ground, the site was little changed in one hundred years. Close to the road is a simple stone monument, bearing a grey metal plaque, commemorating the soldiers of the 1st Australian Mining Company who died at Hill 60.

The hill itself was man-made, the result of earth taken out of a cutting when the railway was first laid in the 1860s, and this railway line made the hill one of strategic importance during the war. Mines were laid under the German lines first in 1915 and then later in 1917 during the Battle of Messines. Caterpillar Crater, a result of one of the mines is now a water filled pool, where frogs croaked noisily from the reeds, with a single tall tree growing at the edge of the water and the perimeter of the lip of the crater surrounded by trees. We explored the area of the front line that has remained well preserved, stepping through a landscape still bearing the impressions of shell holes and trenches and a concrete bunker, now half buried and leaning to one side. The trees have regrown here but at the time of the First World War it was a muddy scene, pockmarked with shell holes and craters, treeless except for naked shattered trunks, and scattered with dead soldiers from both sides. Photographs displayed on the information boards illustrated just how close the two opposing front lines had been: little more than

20 yards apart in places. Just as we were returning to the bikes a school party was arriving, a group from Scotland, one of many school groups we encountered during the week.

From Hill 60 we cycled south and west, passing more cemeteries located along quiet country lanes. On the outskirts of the village of St Eloi we came to another crater that was marked as a point of interest on our map. Unfortunately it appeared to be on private land and was now surrounded by a fence, a large metal gate prevented access. Unknown to us at the time we were close to where one of our relatives had been involved in the skirmishes that had taken place here in the early spring of 1916 when British troops had attempted to capture the mound known as The Bluff.

Disappointed not to have seen the crater we carried on down the road until we reached a small turn off to the left. We were on land that in November 1914 had been on the German front line. This was Bayernwald, a small elevated woodland that had been named after the Bavarian troops of the German army that had been stationed here during the Battle of Messines. And the preserved features we had come to see were German trenches. Now just ten per cent of these remain, a series of them, running through a small area that today faced open fields to the northwest and a patch of woodland to the southeast. This un-staffed, small open air museum was carefully fenced off and a turnstile and automatic gate barred entry to anyone without a ticket. We didn't have a ticket. Tickets could be purchased from the Tourist Information Centre in Kemmel. We weren't going to cycle all the way there and back just for a ticket. But at the same time we did not want to miss one of the best preserved stretches of trenches, either German or Allied, on the entire Western Front. We had clearly not been the only people to arrive unprepared and ticketless. About fifty feet from the gate someone had pulled up a section of the fence, leaving a gap just large enough to wriggle under. We were faced with a moral dilemma.

"I'm game if you are," I said to Mike.

There was no one in sight. Mike wriggled under the fence.

"Mind that bird muck," he said as he emerged the other side and held the fence as I began to squirm under it.

"I'm more concerned about my shoulder and arm than the bird poo," I replied, wriggling around and trying not to drag my arm through the grass and dried earth.

Dusting ourselves off we read the information boards before walking down into the trenches. Many of the trenches and dugouts we were to come across seemed very sanitised, at odds with the reality of the mud, filth, smell, noise and misery of how these places had once been. So much so that at times it was difficult to equate these trenches surrounded by greenery and birdsong with the black and white images of the thigh deep mud, death, explosives and wretchedness that we see in old footage and stills of the Great War. And these German trenches at Bayernwald were no exception. Wide, rough planks lined the floor of the trenches, and sandbags and woven birch and willow branches lined the walls, these were clearly not the originals after over 100 years but faithful representations. At intervals along the trenches we came across bunkers and dug outs; these were dark, damp and oppressive places and it must have been nerve racking to shelter in them during enemy artillery bombardments. In one corner of the site, at the end of one of the trenches was a mine shaft, now flooded but once access to the tunnels that ran under Allied lines. Communication trenches ran back from the front line trenches, meeting up with reserve and supply trenches. And in order to protect against attacking soldiers and against blast, the trenches zigzagged at regular intervals. To risk raising your head above the parapet would have been to risk being shot by an enemy sniper watching across the expanse of no-man's-land but today the view over the top is one of grass, trees and agricultural fields.

So many of the trenches, the shell holes, bunkers and dugouts are gone, filled in by farmers after the war, eager to return to normality, to return to their homes and the land many families had farmed for generations, to return productivity to the land. The woods too have been replanted and the hedgerows. Even entire towns and villages, left in ruins by the conflict, have been rebuilt, many, such as Ypres, faithfully so on the same street pattern and to the same architecture. To such an extent and often with such unswerving accuracy have some places been rebuilt that a person returning later could be forgiven for thinking the destruction had never taken place. So the landscape we were cycling through appeared for much of the time, inevitably, to be little touched by the Great War; although touched it undoubtedly had been, it had since been repaired and reclaimed by both man and nature.

One of the information boards at Bayernwald showed photographs of the German soldiers in the trenches here. In one group, a soldier wearing a splendid moustache sat amongst his comrades. There was nothing other than the moustache to distinguish him from any of his peers. This nondescript man with the moustache would be injured later but would survive. And in subsequent years his splendid facial hair would be trimmed down, reduced to perhaps the most recognisable moustache in history. Of all the millions of men who died in the Great War, Adolf Hitler survived. At the time the photograph had been taken he was serving as a Lance Corporal in the 2nd Bavarian Infantry Regiment. His subsequent rise to Chancellor of Germany and leader of the Third Reich would be in part due to the Treaty of Versailles and its crippling economic effects on Germany.

Country lanes led us past fields where cattle grazed the long grass next to two flooded craters that did not even rate a mention on our map. Next stop on our cycle ride that morning was the Peace Pool in the Spanbroekmolen Mine Crater. This huge crater had been formed during the Battle of Messines by the explosion of one of nineteen mines that had been laid in tunnels under land occupied by the German Army. We walked all around the perimeter, pushing our bikes along a grassy track, unable to see the pool at all for tall trees and dense shrubs. It was only when we arrived within feet of where we had left the road that we came across the entrance.

"It's always good to have a break from cycling," I commented wryly. "And take the bikes for a walk."

Mike grinned and we wheeled the bikes through the gate and propped them against a tree before making our way up a short flight of steps to the rim of the crater from where we could look down at the lily pads covering the water at the edges of the pond. Fish jumped in the water, a blackbird sang from a nearby tree, a wood pigeon cooed monotonously and two retired English couples sitting close to the bank whispered a respectful conversation. Unlike the other mines that were detonated on 7th June 1917 at the beginning of the battle, this one did not explode immediately. Something went wrong and the explosion was delayed by 15 seconds. Advancing Allied troops had reached here at just the wrong time and many were killed. The crater left by the explosion measured 129 metres in diameter and was more than 12 metres deep. It was yet another peaceful, contemplative place that bore little resemblance to the time and space of its creation.

The Battle of Messines began on 7th July 1917 and would last for a week, but careful preparation had begun 18 months previously and included the digging of tunnels stretching deep and far under the German held ground, into which explosives would be laid. The British and New Zealand forces commenced the assault with the detonation of 19 mines laid under German lines stretching along the ridge between Ploegsteert in the south and Hill 60 in the north. Messines itself is a small city, not a fact you are aware of when cycling through, it had the impression of yet another small, quaint Belgian town. But in 1914 it had the bad luck of being strategically placed on high ground and as a consequence suffered much during the war. For three years the Germans successfully held this high ground but the Allies had long had their sights on this important elevated position and in just one week the Allies achieved their objectives. The Battle of Messines is regarded as one of the most successful for the Allies during the entire war. But more battles were to follow and they would not all have the same outcome.

The coach full of school children that had been at Hill 60 earlier in the morning arrived just as we were leaving the Peace Pool. The guide was getting them all to line up along the edge of the road, facing out, down the hill and with a view of the landscape laid out before them.

"Why have I got you all to stand in a line here?" he asked, as we unlocked the bicycles.

"For the view?" came one tentative reply.

"Yes!" exclaimed the guide with a passion that far outweighed the enthusiasm of his audience. "This is a great vantage point..."

We moved on, leaving the guide explaining why a view of that farm, those cows and the town in the distance had been relevant one hundred years ago. We stopped a short time later at Messines Ridge Cemetery. This is the resting place of over 1500 Commonwealth soldiers, nearly one third of who could not be identified. We were to see so many gravestones bearing simply the inscriptions 'A soldier of the Great War' and 'Known unto God' at all the cemeteries we visited. In some cases the regiment of the dead soldier had been know, presumably from either the location of his death or scraps of uniform that remained; in those cases the graves were also carved with the name of the regiment and the regimental badge. How many families had suffered the added agony of knowing that their dead sons had not been identified? The reason for this high proportion of unknown remains can be explained by the fact that many of the impromptu burial plots in the surrounding area were moved to this cemetery following the end of the war. At the entrance to this cemetery was a monument to the missing men of New Zealand who had fought in the Battle of Messines. 839 of them died and have no known grave. How many families had suffered this equal agony?

We stopped in Mesen, the Belgian spelling of Messines, to buy some salad, fruit and cake for lunch. Packing the food into our panniers we cycled the short distance to the Irish Tower. Of the many memorials we saw dotted through the Western Front, one of the most unique and outstanding was the Irish Peace Tower just on the edge of Mesen. It is located in the Island of Ireland Peace Park and when we arrived employees of the Commonwealth War Graves Commission were just on a lunch break from strimming the grass and pruning the shrubbery. The tower itself, unlike so many of the First World War monuments is made not of limestone, brick or marble but of stone taken from a demolished workhouse in Ireland and transported to Belgium to be rebuilt into a replica of an eighth century Irish tower. It stands some 33 metres high and is dedicated to all the soldiers from Ireland who lost their lives fighting for Britain during the Great War. Seeing it was like stepping into County Wicklow where I had once seen an almost identical tower. Thought had gone into the design of the tower, not just the choice of its shape but into the symbolism. By virtue of its clever design and the positioning of the small, sparse windows light only penetrates the tower on the eleventh hour of the eleventh day of the eleventh month.

The sun shone down as we sat eating our lunch in the landscaped park. As well as some healthy salad and fruit we had indulged in puff pastry tarts filled with a gooey chocolate concoction and generously dusted with icing sugar. Mike munched happily, dropping icing sugar all over himself before inhaling some, sneezing and spraying more white dust all over his legs and the bike. I raised an eyebrow in amusement and exasperation as I looked at him.

"You're covered in icing sugar!"

He began rubbing it in. "That better?"

"Hm, marginally," I replied. "But you've got a white moustache – as opposed to your usual grey one!"

Our cue to leave came with the arrival of two large coaches decanting two large groups of English school children who swarmed across the peace park being anything but peaceful. We loaded the litter onto the bikes, wheeled them out of the cemetery and headed south. Within minutes we reached another cemetery and its extension, facing one another across a wide road. This was the Berks Cemetery and amongst its many graves we found one soldier, a Rifleman with the King's Royal Rifle Corps. His grave stopped us in our tracks. This soldier had died in June 1916, aged just sixteen. In the same cemetery, situated close to the back perimeter wall were three headstones marking the graves of three German soldiers. They were, rightly, equally well cared for, equally well maintained and equally respected. These men had all died in 1917 and one of them was an unknown soldier: 'Ein unbekannter Deutscher Krieger' read the inscription.

Just behind this cemetery was Ploegsteert Wood and it was here that one of the most remarked upon and poignant events of the First World War occurred. The 1914 Christmas Day truce is a famous part of the First World War. Soldiers of opposing armies coming together in no-man's-land to talk, share rations and play football. The commanding officers on both sides ensured it never happened again. But there were other smaller acts of humanity and compassion in the carnage of the Great War that are often overlooked. A German prisoner being treated by a British Army doctor. A Tommy sharing his water ration with a captured German soldier. An English soldier administering first aid to a German prisoner. If only these small acts of compassion by enemies on the Front Line could have been magnified and extended to the commanding officers of both sides, perhaps the war really would have been over by Christmas.

The morning had been taken up with a slow journey along the Front and frequent stops to visit the points of interest. The afternoon was a contrast of putting miles under our wheels. We stopped on one country lane, making use of the shade presented by a small copse of roadside trees whilst we applied more sunscreen and checked the map. Hidden amongst this circular copse was a small mound and atop the mound a cross with a carving of a life sized Christ. Subtle, hidden and yet from the look of it not forgotten, it was another monument to yet another battle of the Great War.

We cycled through villages where pavement cafes tantalised us with the smell of frites. In one village alternating beds of white and red roses lined the pavements; the evocative scent reminded me of the hot summers of my childhood and my mum's roses in her small terraced house garden. We crossed the border into France and into the town of Armentieres with its pretty buildings and a church in the centre of the town. There had been no official sign that we had even crossed the border, just a dawning awareness that the road signs were now in French and that the cycle path provision was not as good as it had been. Where they existed at all the cycle paths were now much narrower lanes at the side of the road, rather than separated from the carriageway, and there was much broken glass and gravel which we attempted to avoid as best we could.

In Belgium we had been struck by how vehicles gave way to bicycles at roundabouts: whether it be entering or exiting, we seemed to have priority. It caught us out at first as we would pause to give way to traffic already on the roundabout, only to find the traffic was stopping to let us pull out. Where cycle lanes along the pavement crossed side roads, again we had priority. I'm sure we left a trail of bemused if not impatient drivers in our wake before we got used to this unaccustomed precedence. On crossing into France this had changed and having just got used to one system we then fell foul of another type of precedence: priorité a droite. To our British road users' mind-set cars entering the main road from a side road on the right must automatically give way. Not so to the French mind-set and rules of the road. To make things even more confusing, this system did not work at every junction and despite trying to figure out the pattern of circumstances when priorité a droite did come into play we never quite worked it out. The result was at times a nerve wracking experience as we swerved around cars pulling out in front of us, or slammed on the brakes to avoid them, or simply cycled in front of them causing more than a few irate stares and Gaelic shrugs.

Mike was resorting more and more frequently to the GPS on his mobile to navigate us through the urban areas and from one busy, sprawling town to the next. But this was not an easy process, made all the more time consuming as he did not have a handle bar mount for the phone.

"You need one of those handle bar mounts for the phone!" I would frequently remark.

"Yes, I'll have to see about getting one," he would reply before contorting round to open a pannier and fish out his phone.

The next few minutes would always pan out the same. He would mutter, jab at the phone, lift his head to orientate himself with what we were seeing and what the phone was telling him and then, invariably...

"No! We're not there! Catch up will you!"

I would then ask where we needed to be. To which I would get one of two responses. He would either be too engrossed in the GPS to even realise I had spoken, pandas on roller skates had danced around us, a streaker had run past or a UFO had landed and taken me to their leader. Or alternatively he would say something in French that I had no idea how to spell. I would then glance around and say something like 'there's a road sign over there pointing to... er... Erkin... jem... hhe... Erkinjemhahumm... er lice.'

At which point Mike would look up, read the road sign I was pointing at and say something that bore no resemblance to what I had just said but with a French accent. Adding, "Thanks, yes, that's helpful. I know which way we need to go now."

My French is woefully inadequate and a source of some shame and embarrassment to me. But my map reading is probably even worse so I am more than happy to leave both to Mike. And so is he.

After a few wrong turns we found our way to the towpath at the side of a large canal. Just one problem. The towpath was closed for some sort of building work. Mike muttered something and contorted himself to get his phone.

"You need one of those handle bar mounts for the phone!"

We retraced our route, turned down a residential street, cycled round in a big loop passing some nice houses with lovely gardens and then ended up back where we started. Mike muttered something and contorted himself to get his phone. I kept my mouth shut. We moved off, I caught my shin on the end of one of the front mud guard supports and blood began to trickle down my leg. We got lost again. Mike... oh, you get the picture! We set off again, turning right this time, I caught my other shin on the end of the other support for the front mud guard and that too began to bleed. Originally the support ends had had a little protective rubber cap on but at some point I had caught them with my toe and knocked them off. I really ought to get round to replacing them, or buying shin pads. Or maybe a full suit of armour would be better.

When we eventually found access onto the canal towpath just fifty yards away from where it had been closed, having pushed the bikes through a pleasant park, Mike noticed my legs were bleeding.

"What have you done now?" he asked with concern, a sigh and an eye roll.

"Bit of a mishap. Twice," I replied sheepishly. "Still, at least I stayed on the bike!"

The next few sunny miles were along the wide towpath of this even wider canal. Not like my local Leeds and Liverpool, this canal for one thing was not full of litter, toilet bowls, armchairs or dustbins, (not that the entire length of the Leeds and Liverpool is like that, just some bits). A large cargo barge sailed past us, its sides and deck displayed 'flammable' signs as it carried its cargo of oil towards the coast. Another barge, with a collection of bicycles cluttering the rear deck, was carrying small shipping containers. It is refreshing to see that canals and the larger rivers in continental Europe are still used in this way. Of more interest to us though was the wildlife that lived around this busy canal. A cormorant bobbed up with a wriggling fish in its beak. Coots and their young pipped and piped from closer to the bank, swans and their cygnets glided by and mallards with their baker's dozen of ducklings dabbled and quacked. We cycled this stretch of the canal from near the town of Don all the way to just before Lens, leaving the canal when we reached Vendi le Vieil. Unfortunately the navigating immediately proved challenging again, not helped when we had to carry the bikes up a long flight of steps, along a road that crossed the railway line and then down another flight of steps to join another road on the other side of the tracks. I say we, I mean Mike, my left shoulder was not capable of lifting anything so poor Mike had to heave both laden bikes up and then down the two flights of steps in the sweltering heat of late afternoon.

We cycled down a quiet road lined with terraced houses of red brick. They were typical of this former coal mining area but unusual for the region as a whole. Many of the houses had a rundown air about them and it was not the most picturesque part of our journey. But this was the approach to the town of Lens, in what had once been an important coal mining region. Pyramidal slag heaps towered above the surroundings. Many of them had been there since before the First World War and they can be seen in old photographs of the battlefields. It was like a French industrial version of Egypt, these pyramidal slag heaps were huge and we were still able to see them many miles later.

It was a hot afternoon and we continued to have frequent stops to gulp down water and apply sunscreen. From Lens we found ourselves on a busy main road climbing up Vimy Ridge. This was the largest, longest, steepest ascent of our entire cycle ride and yet we would have barely considered it a hill of any significance had it been in Britain. But in this relatively flat part of northern Europe Vimy Ridge had been a strategic vantage point and much fought over during the First World War. Atop the centre of the ridge, the white twin towers of the Canadian Memorial had been visible for some miles, shining in the strong late afternoon sunshine. We cycled along the top of the ridge on a quiet road through an avenue of maple trees, significant as the maple is the emblem of Canada.

Shortly after reaching the top of the ridge we had followed the road over a cutting where below us traffic hurtled along on a new highway. I was disappointed to find Vimy Ridge cut through by a modern motorway. This rude highway slicing through the site of the old battleground is nothing new, a similar road had cut through Messines Ridge, progress and growth continue despite what had once occurred here. Where once the sound of bird song was obliterated by the sound of heavy artillery, detonating mines, machine guns and the screams of wounded and dying men, today the sound of bird song competes against the roaring backdrop of articulated lorries, trucks and cars hurtling between Paris and Calais. Now travellers rush to their destinations, one hundred years ago men rushed to their deaths. What had I been expecting? The entire Western Front to be a preserved landscape of humps and craters, trenches and bunkers neatly landscaped and grassed over, trees replanted, respectful preservation of a major battle site and grave to untold thousands of lost men? Life inevitably goes on, modern day life; it would not be possible to preserve every square metre of battleground. But a motorway, modern, black tarmac and white lines, carrying speeding vehicles into their daily lives of work, shopping, school, holiday, was not how I had pictured the clichéd image we are fed of poppy-covered Flanders fields. It was more than a disappointment, it was an intrusion but I knew I was over-reacting.

Where I found the busy new road a negative, there were also positives for today the Ridge is once more covered with trees as it was before the devastation of the War, but 100 years ago all vegetation had been blasted off the face of the hill. As we cycled further along the ridge the avenue of maples turned into woodland bordering both sides of the road before we emerged into an open area where craters and shell holes, now grown over with grass, were still visible as humps and pits in the pockmarked landscape. In parts of the wood and grassland bordering the road and the monument there remains much unexploded ordnance and the area was surrounded by a low wire barrier with red warning signs hanging from the wire: 'Danger: Undetonated Explosives'. It was a clear reminder that this landscape, these battle grounds can still turn up dangerous relics of the past. Throughout the Western Front unexploded ordnance is a constant nuisance for farmers who frequently unearth rusty, pitted shells that still have the power to maim and kill. We were to come across more of these warning signs at Beaumont Hamel, although it seemed sheep were considered either less likely to set off an explosion or worth risking as there, amongst other places, sheep are left to graze on the danger areas.

The monument at Vimy Ridge stands tall and proud at the edge of the ridge and can be seen for miles around. Set behind it and lower down the back of the ridge are various car parks, footpaths and a visitor centre in the Canadian Memorial Park. The whole area the park stands on was given to Canada by the French in 1922, a thank you for the sacrifice made by the Canadian soldiers who fought here during the Battle of Arras (more of that particular battle later). There are preserved trenches, one of the few places along the entire Western Front where this is the case; and it was amazing to see how close the two sides were, in some places little more than 30 feet. The park contains the now grass covered craters and shell holes I had been expecting and 11,285 Canadian trees and shrubs that I had not. Each tree or shrub represents one Canadian soldier who died fighting in the war but whose body was never found. We arrived too late for the visitor information centre. In a week we simply could not see everything and on the Western Front there is so much, too much to see, I am sure we would return.

Leaving the bikes we walked up the gravelled path to the Canadian National Vimy Memorial, at that time in the afternoon the visiting crowds, many of them Canadian, had gone, just a few stragglers remained, strolling round the monument and taking in the lists of names engraved on the memorial. A list that runs to 11,285 missing soldiers. That list is not the final number, a further 6998 missing Canadian soldiers are listed on the Menin Gate. In total 66,000 Canadians lost their lives in the First World War. The Vimy Memorial pays tribute to them all and stands nearly fifty metres high. Atop the two limestone columns are the Canadian maple leaf and the French fleur-de-lys. At the bottom of the towers and in the centre is a carved figure, several times life-size, of a grieving woman, Canada mourning for her lost sons. Of all the monuments we saw on this northern part of the Western Front this is without doubt the most outstanding. It shone in the strong sunlight, glaring and bright, a stark contrast to the grey skies and sleet the Canadian troops faced on Easter Monday in April 1917 as they began their attack.

From Vimy Ridge it was downhill to Arras and our hotel for the night. We still had some miles to go and as we descended the ridge and headed south on more quiet roads we soon came to another cemetery, this time a German one which seemed to have more graves than any cemetery we had seen so far. We cycled around the rear perimeter of the cemetery to reach the main road to Arras. Reaching the outskirts of this large town we hit the rush hour traffic and were faced with a long slog through the busy town along a confusion of roads, dual carriageways, shopping streets and cycle lanes. We needed eyes everywhere as Mike tried to navigate and I tried to follow him whilst both of us watched out for cars priorité a droite-ing and pedestrians stepping into the road. The early evening rush hour was showing no signs of dwindling as we reach the north eastern edge of Arras, now on the lookout for a supermarket to buy something for an evening meal and for our hotel. We were on a suburban street, wide with two lanes on each side and lots of parked cars, when we passed a small convenience store. It looked too small to offer much in the way of fresh bread, salads and fruit so we continued. Before long we had reached our hotel, set back down a side road and right on the edge of town. Mike checked his phone.

"There's a supermarket not far down this road," he said. "The phone reckons five minutes by bike."

"We could try that," I replied. "Go now and then register in the hotel afterwards."

"Don't you want to freshen up first?"

"Not really. I won't feel like coming out once we've gone in and had a shower and a cuppa."

"Shoulder bothering you?" he asked, as I tried to move my arm without wincing.

"Well, it's an improvement on yesterday, I've been able to reach the brake hood this afternoon. By tomorrow I might be changing gear," I added with a hopeful smirk.

We set off in the direction of the supermarket down a busy dual carriageway. We turned left at a busy crossroads and then along a cycle path into what appeared to be an industrial estate.

"I'm not trusting this," Mike remarked grumpily.

He was right not to. The supermarket the sat nav had brought us to was large. It was sure to have everything: bread, meat, salad, wine, beer, security gates. Security gates? On a supermarket? No, on a distribution warehouse for a supermarket.

Mike went into melt down. A bit unreasonable I thought considering it wasn't him with the painful shoulder. A sense of humour failure of epic proportions followed. There were several minutes of Tourette-like language. Much questioning of a sat nav's ability to make any kind of reasonable judgement. Several more minutes of colourful, non-politically correct cursing. And then he paused for breath.

"Never mind," I interjected into the gap. "It's not that far back to the convenience store. We'll be able to get something there."

It didn't take me long to say that, but long enough apparently for him to draw breath and begin another rant.

"Come on! This isn't helping! Me or my shoulder," I muttered as I cycled off back the way we had come.

Arriving at the store we began to secure our bikes to a drain pipe outside. Mike was still simmering, a bit like my shoulder. I just wanted to get in, get some food, get to our hotel and get in the shower. As we struggled to fit the lock through both bikes we heard a voice.

"Bring zem in!"

We looked round to see the owner of the shop, an elderly man of Middle Eastern appearance, waving at us and smiling.

"Bring zem in, put zem 'ere," he repeated, pointing to a stack of pallets immediately inside the door. "Zee will be safe. I will watch zem."

Thanking him excessively we wheeled the bikes into the shop, abandoned them where he had indicated and grabbed a basket. Mike head for the beer section, I headed for the chocolate section, somewhere in between we found the fresh food aisle and added bananas, sliced chorizo, tomatoes and a bag of salad leaves to the beer, diet coke, chocolate and crisps we had already grabbed. Bread was more of a problem. The baguettes had long since gone and the only options were a large sliced loaf (yes we were hungry but not that hungry) and some seeded burger buns.

"They'll do," Mike said, grabbing a pack of four and heading for the biscuit aisle.

We joined a queue that seemed to consist of other tourists as well as locals, all of whom the friendly shopkeeper chatted to as he rang up their shopping. Two minutes later we were cramming our purchases into the panniers and strapping the bottles of beer and coke onto the top of the pannier racks. With the bread rolls and the bag of salad carefully placed just in the tops of the panniers where they wouldn't get too squashed we set off to the hotel. We had barely gone a minute down the road, with me in the lead, when I heard a crash and a shout behind me. Fearing the worst I stopped and turned round. Mike was laughing and leaping off his bike. The bag of salad had slipped out of his pannier and landed in the middle of the road. He dashed back to retrieve it before an oncoming car ran over the healthy part of our feast.

Two sweaty, laughing minutes later we arrived at the hotel. It was a typical no-frills business hotel but cheap and cheerful and had got good reviews for its buffet breakfast, always a selling point as far as I was concerned. Leaving Mike outside with the bikes I went in to register. But I wasn't confident in my French, mainly because I didn't have any, so had no choice but to hope someone in reception would understand a little English if nothing else.

"Parlais vous..." I began and then hesitated.

Hang on, I wasn't about to make that mistake again! In Nice a few years ago I had asked in French if the person behind the desk had spoken French. It had caused much amusement both to the staff and to Mike, especially when the answer had been "Do you mean English?"

"...er Anglais?" I added after thinking it through.

"A little," came the reply.

A little turned out to be rather a lot. Soon I had registered and been shown where we could store the bikes, issued with a swipe card for our room and given precise directions, in English, where to find our room. We removed the panniers and the bottles from our bikes, wheeled the bikes into an empty seminar room and locked them together, then headed up a flight of stairs to our first floor room. It was hot and stuffy and the first thing we did was throw open the window. The sounds of a busy road, laughter from a group of businessmen sitting on the patio below and a television in another room with an equally wide open window drifted into our room. But we didn't care. We collapsed onto the bed not knowing whether to sit down, shower or have a drink first. In the end we had a drink while Mike attempted to help me out of my cycling top without moving my shoulder. Not an easy task.

"Argh!" I squealed.

"Sorry, I'm trying to be careful. Was that your shoulder?"

"No, my top got stuck on my nose," I mumbled. "I thought you were going to rip my nose off."

Some more wrangling ensued and more squealing on my part before I parted company with my cycling top. I went into the bathroom to switch on the shower and promptly banged my grazed arm on the door handle. It was my turn to have a sense of humour failure.

"Ooh, are you okay?" Mike asked with concern.

"I've been better," I replied through gritted teeth.

Once in the shower the graze stung less than I was anticipating but once out of the shower and attempting to operate a towel one handed I banged my arm on the door again. I managed to wrap the towel round me, putting on clothes was too painful an effort, and headed out of the bathroom at which point I banged my arm on the door handle for a third time. Slow learner.

Mike was setting out the food on the desk and peering quizzically at the high spec coffee maker and muttering something about over engineering and what was wrong with a kettle for goodness sake.

"You better set the alarm for extra early if you're thinking of having a coffee in the morning," I said as I watched him.

"I don't think I'll bother!"

We ate the food whilst watching the sky outside becoming progressively blacker as thunder clouds built up. Low rumbles began to grow increasingly loud.

"I better move our trainers," Mike said, going over to the window and reaching out to bring in our footwear from the wide windowsill.

Our just washed socks had already been brought inside when the wind had begun to pick up. The last thing we (and possibly the businessmen below) wanted was for our socks to be blown onto the patio. Whilst Mike was picking our trainers off the windowsill I was picking sesame seeds off my legs, it seemed most of the seeds had dropped off the buns before reaching my mouth.

We went to bed a little after ten o'clock, after the 66 mile day in the sultry heat we were tired. Within minutes the thunder changed from distant rumbles to loud and ever-nearer claps, lightning flashed across the sky and rain pelted down in torrents. Unable to sleep we got up and watched the thunderstorm. I was reminded of the storm my friend Chris and I had got up to watch one night when we had been walking the South West Coast Path many years ago. There is something about a powerful electrical storm that is mesmerising. Soon a river of rain water was washing down the gutters, flooding the road and sweeping across the car park. We went to bed and fell asleep long before the storm was over.

Tuesday 29th May 2018. 31 miles.

Sun was streaming into the window helping to dry two pairs of cycling shorts and tops that were hanging from the curtain rail. Early morning traffic on the busy dual carriageway was just building up to an intrusive rumble in the background and on the roof of the hotel a blackbird was singing. We had a shorter day that day, just 31 miles to our next stop at Albert but there would be plenty of points of interest on the way.

It had been a hot and sticky night but I was loath to attempt the painful ritual of another shower and the contortions of trying to wash and dry myself with my shoulder which seemed to have stiffened up overnight. Sleeping too was proving difficult as I was unable to lie on my left side, my default sleeping position, and found myself spending much of the night on my back, snoring and waking both myself and Mike up as a result. Wincing, I crawled out of bed and began the equally painful ritual of trying to dress. Mike meanwhile was attempting to operate the fancy coffee machine.

"Sod it," I heard him mutter as I emerged from the bathroom. "Let's go and get breakfast."

The hotel dining room was nearly empty when we arrived, a couple of businessmen occupied two tables and a waitress hovered around looking short of something to do. I headed for the selection of yoghurt and cereal whilst Mike made a beeline for the coffee which he declared to be very good. The same could not be said of the tea and I persevered with something lurking in a small mesh bag calling itself 'breakfast tea' but which after five minutes steeping in a small cup of hot water steadfastly refused to resemble anything other than a small cup of hot water. I gave up and switched to orange juice. Bread, croissants, rich butter, jams and chocolate spread were all going down well when on my third trip to the buffet table I discovered sausages and bacon. They went down well too.

"Where did you get those from?" Mike asked as I plonked a plate down on the table with two rashers of bacon and a couple of pork sausages.

"Under the metal lids," I replied, pointing to the end of the buffet.

"You're risking French sausage? After our experience in Provence?" he said sceptically, referring to a holiday a few years ago when we had chosen a meaty looking sausage in the supermarket only to discover on cooking it that it not only smelt of faeces but it tasted of them too. Closer inspection had revealed it to contain nothing but the lower digestive tract of pigs.

"This one neither smells nor taste of poo!"

"Oh I might try some then."

Replete with breakfast we returned to our room, changed into our cycling clothes and packed up the panniers. I had been too tired the previous evening to pay much attention to the room we had left our bikes in. That morning I noticed that there was a strong smell of cigarette smoke, a lot of dirty cups dumped on one table and vast quantities of hair trimmings littering the floor. It looked like the room had been hosting a particularly slovenly hairdressers' conference.

We cycled into the main part of Arras and navigated our way past a couple of supermarkets we'd not seen the evening before until we reached the visitor centre at Wellington Tunnels, named after the city in New Zealand from which many of the men who dug them came. Back in Roman times the area where Arras now stands was quarried for its stone and this quarrying continued down the centuries to leave a subterranean system of tunnels, shafts and galleries. When the First World War broke out the British Army made use of the existing network of tunnels, widening and extending them as part of the war effort. Today some of The Wellington Tunnels are now a carefully preserved museum, with an interactive visitor centre popular with tourists and school groups. We were keen to see the tunnels, and the visitor centre runs regular guided tours throughout the day where you can walk through the tunnels and see the stairs leading out into the open air up which the Canadians soldiers walked to emerge into the area of land in front of the German trenches.

A school group had been booked in to take the first tour of the day and places are limited so we signed on for the 11 o'clock tour and spent the next hour exploring the displays of artefacts recovered from the tunnels, the uniforms of the French, German and Commonwealth soldiers, the armaments, the kit issued to the different soldiers, and letters, mementoes and keepsakes. We sat in the dark watching an emotionally charged film using original footage of the conflict that explained the timeline and the Battle of Arras. We browsed the literature, avoided the souvenirs and waited as more people arrived and booked onto the 11 a.m. tour.

A party of Dutch pensioners arrived, were guided through the till by their group leader and began selecting hard hats in preparation for the tour of the tunnels. The Dutch must have a collective fear of head lice, as every member of the group donned a disposable hair net before plonking on a hard hat designed in the shape and style of a Tommies' helmet. We had simply stuck the helmets on our heads as had the rest of the British tourists.

With just a few minutes to spare before our tour was due to begin an English couple arrived. Brash, loud and with a Home Counties accent the woman addressed the young man on the reception desk with a voice that could have cut through an aerial bombardment.

"Do you give a discount for pensioners?" she demanded.

"No, madam," the startled member of staff replied. "I am sorry we do not."

Mike and I exchanged a glance. The woman was dressed in an elegant trouser suit that was clearly more Selfridges than Sainsburys. The entrance fee was a modest seven Euros. How much cheaper did she want it?

Mike rolled his eyes and I instantly went into inverted snob mode and as the woman tutted loudly and asked if they took American Express.

"How much cheaper does she want it?" I exclaimed. "She'll be asking if they give Nectar points next!"

"She doesn't look the type to collect Nectar points!" Mike muttered.

As the eleventh hour approached a guide called the visitors together, collected our tickets and began to introduce himself and explain a little about the Tunnels tour. His English was perfect as he switched between that and his native French. Following his instructions we trailed in his wake through some doors and across a concrete floor to a lift where all nineteen of us squeezed in and descended to the tunnels. Prior to the Battle of Arras the old tunnel workings had been enlarged and improved, and in the hour long tour of the tunnels that followed our descent the guide explained in detail, with the aid of video footage projected onto the walls and some visual remnants in the tunnels and chambers, how the tunnels had been dug and their importance in the battle. We were led past an old well, side chambers were men had slept in rough wooden bunk beds, chambers used for storage, past rough-hewn walls still bearing the hand written signs pointing to the latrines or, most eerie of all to 'Number 10 Exit' and 'Circular Trench'. It was moving to think some of the last feet to walk past those signs over 100 years ago had been emerging into daylight in front of the German Front line.

By 1917 the German Army had come to believe they would be unable to withstand another battle on the scale of The Somme. Seeking to strengthen the remaining positions they knew they could more easily defend, the German Army began a strategic withdrawal to the Siegfried-Stellung or Hindenburg Line as the British called it. The line ran from near Arras south and east towards Soissons. As they retreated the Germans employed a scorched earth policy. Towns, villages and farms were raised to the ground, wells poisoned and booby traps laid. The move took the Allies by surprise. The British Army had been intending to attack the parts of the Front the Germans had just left, instead a change of plan was called for and on 9th April the British Army with the support of several Canadian divisions attacked Arras. The Canadians successfully captured Vimy Ridge, but attack and counter attack followed until by the end of May a British unit broke through part of the Hindenburg Line. While all this had been going on, to the south the French Army had launched an attack at Chemin des Dames. After two weeks of fighting, despite some early success, there had been no breakthrough and the French Army was suffering increasingly heavy losses. Mutinies began to break out, soldiers refused to return to the Front and fight.

The Grimsby Chums another Pals Battalion (10th Battalion Lincolnshire Regiment) had been formed by the former headmaster of Winteringham Secondary School. In a patriotic act so typical of the time, the headmaster no doubt thought he was helping his boys do their bit for King and Country. They fought together and they died together on Easter Monday 1917; and in June 2001 twenty of their bodies were discovered together in a mass grave near Arras, arms linked and still wearing their boots.

The Battle of Vimy Ridge was part of the Battle of Arras and Vimy was attacked by four Canadian Divisions, a country that at the time was still part of the British Empire. The German Army holding the high ground of the ridge, known as The Pimple, had the upper hand and with fortified trenches and bunkers this had proved impenetrable up until this point. But despite this the Canadians were to prove successful, and this success was due in large part to the Wellington Tunnels. Prior to the assault this network of tunnels had been dug, extending the old underground quarries. The stable nature of the soft chalk of the region proved ideal for tunnelling. Both sides had made networks of tunnels and in earlier months the Germans had out-mined the French but the tables were turned when British and Commonwealth miners took over from their Allies; and by spring of 1916 they were mining both offensively and strategically to stop the Germans' advancing their own tunnels. Eventually the British tunnels ran for a total length of over seven miles.

I had imagined the tunnels to be narrow passages, where tunnellers and engineers would have to squeeze through the claustrophobic burrows but the reality was far different. The Wellington Tunnels were far more than cramped, narrow passageways and were instead more like a complex warren of channels and chambers: some tunnels contained hospitals, ammunition stores, communications centres and even light railways. The tunnels would be used to advance Allied soldiers into position close to the

German line, from which they would emerge at the beginning of the attack, bypassing No Man's Land and the scything machine gunfire.

The Battle of Vimy Ridge began on Easter Monday, 9th April 1917, and lasted until the 12th. Immediately before the attack British sappers laid thirteen mines under the German positions. But if this is sounding reminiscent of The Somme, think again. Hard lessons had been learnt from The Somme on the effects of mines and the craters they created which then posed problems for advancing Allied troops. As a result some of the mines were removed or not detonated at all along the sector over which the Canadians would advance. Eventually just a small handful of mines were detonated before the attack. The tactics of tunnels worked, the Battle of Arras began with a huge explosion and 24,000 men emerged from their hiding places in the tunnels directly in front of the German front line trench.

The Battle of Vimy Ridge came to be regarded as the first indisputable success by British and Commonwealth forces in trench warfare. But despite the success of the Battle of Vimy Ridge, it was only a small part of the Battle of Arras. The British Army and its supporting armies of the Commonwealth were on their own and things were beginning to stall at Arras. Five and half weeks after the Battle of Arras began it ended. Little had been achieved at a cost of 159,000 British lives.

As we walked through those cold, cavernous tunnels we could see graffiti on the walls, carved out by the men who had made them. Five hundred New Zealand men had been employed in the digging of the tunnels, and some of their stories and photographs are now displayed on the entry way to the museum. Not just any men had been selected to do this dangerous and vital work, the companies of men digging the tunnels consisted of mainly coal and gold miners, experts in their field. Less well known and celebrated are the Yorkshire bantams, the miners of the Yorkshire coal fields who had been too short to be enlisted in the army, these men of under five feet three inches had been keen to do their bit for King and country and found themselves transported from the black, dusty coalfaces of Yorkshire to the white, dusty chalk caverns of France.

The tunnels had been used as air raid shelters during the Second World War and then closed up. Some had subsequently collapsed. The tunnels then lay undisturbed for decades but in the 1990s one local archaeologist began investigating them. The result is a stunning museum and monument, a reminder of the effort and sacrifice and suffering undertaken by men from across the Commonwealth in the effort to win the First World War.

At midday we emerged from the tunnels, removed audio headsets and helmets and returned to our bikes. The sun seemed especially bright after the hour spent underground and we exchanged specs for sun glasses before cycling off through the suburbs into the countryside towards Albert. We cycled on main roads away from the city, passing verges covered with large red poppies, past fields of oil seed rape, potatoes and the emerging shoots of sweetcorn. The flat landscape of Flanders had been replaced by gently rolling countryside, there were still no large hills of significance but we were now looking across valleys and low hills instead of the miles of level plains we had cycled through previously. For a main road there was refreshingly little traffic, although the occasional large truck would rumble past every five or ten minutes or so, throwing up dust clouds from the drying soil that had been washed off the fields in the previous night's heavy storm. For a couple of miles a white monument had been visible in the distance, towering over the surrounding fields. Another memorial? No, its true purpose was revealed as we drew closer and were able to see the large letters spelling out the name of a company. This towering structure formed part of a sugar refinery. It seemed to mock the other towering monuments we had come across.

Before leaving Arras Mike had programmed the sat nav on his phone to plot out a cycle-specific route to Albert, our stop for the next two nights. But modern technology was proving to have a mind of its own. Leaving the main road we followed the phone's directions down a pleasant minor road before turning onto an even more minor road which quickly deteriorated into a rutted track running between fields. Thanks to the storm the fields seemed to have invaded the track, the surface of which was flooded with patches of mud and gravel. Our wheels and our bikes were covered in mud within seconds, clogging the gears and the mud guards. It was easy to understand how the Flanders mud had so affected the fighting. As the track followed the line of a natural hollow in the landscape the run off got worse until the bottom of the dip was just a lake of thick, glutinous mud. With Mike muttering about digital technology in a less than positive manner, and extolling the virtues of paper maps (if only we had one for this particular part of our ride!) we dismounted, immediately sinking ankle deep into the mud, heaved the bikes round and retreated to the main road. Once there the sat nav was reprogrammed to 'car' mode and we followed a different route for a few miles before it reconnected us with another minor road we had been attempting to get to before the mud fiasco.

As we reached the village of Bucquoy we found a rarity in France – a supermarket that was open between midday and 2 p.m. We propped the bikes in the insubstantial bike rack, locked them together and went inside to hunt out something for lunch. Tuna salad provided the healthy part of the meal and a religuese, a French version of a chocolate choux bun filled with rich chocolate sauce, decorated with a cream collar and shaped to represent a nun, made up the indulgent part. I didn't trust Mike to cycle with the cream cakes so I took charge of them, placing them carefully into one of my panniers before we cycled down the road looking for somewhere suitable to stop and eat them.

We didn't have far to cycle before we reached the peaceful Queens Cemetery. Leaving the bikes outside we walked round the graves before sitting on the steps of the monument to quietly eat our lunch. The cemetery contained the graves of soldiers who had died in the fighting that occurred in this region between 1916 and 1918. Rows of graves, some known unto God, some identified, all honoured with the graves once again beautifully attended and the grounds respectfully maintained.

As we were finishing our lunch a British family arrived, driving up in a U.K. registered car, parking and then walking along the rows of graves. Three generations of one family: a woman, her partner, their son who was about five years of age and his grandfather. The young boy was carrying a large bouquet of red roses and a single red poppy. They were clearly searching for one particular headstone and before long the overheard conversation between the three adults soon made it clear the grave they had come to visit was the woman's great grandfather.

"He's here," she called to the others.

They gathered round the grave, reading the inscription and each in turn touching the headstone, before, with a prompt from his mum, the little boy laid the flowers on the grass in front of the headstone. Watching, I felt as if I were witness to a private moment, but this family's pilgrimage to the grave of their relative personalised the cemeteries like nothing else could. To see the rows on rows of graves, read the names at so many cemeteries we visited was one thing. To watch a family visiting the grave of their long dead relative linked with the past and with the human, personal cost of the First World War in a way that the thousands of gravestones alone could not.

Thunder was rumbling ominously once again that afternoon and we packed up our litter and moved on. The sat nav was doing its thing again on bicycle mode and soon we found ourselves following a farm track between arable fields where the mud had been washed onto the path. This would have been fine had we been on mountain bikes but the thin walled tyres on our road bikes were beginning to struggle with the soft mud, the ruts and the flinty gravel. Mike consulted his sat nav and after a bit of muttering declared we didn't have very far to go and perhaps it was worth just pushing the bikes. We did this for about half mile, at times squelching through the mud, at times wheeling the bikes along the grassy narrow verge until the track suddenly improved and a metalled surface replaced the mud and flints. Remounting, we cycled off along the track surrounded now by gradually rising land on our left and trees and a hedgerow on the right. The track was now rising and heading for a village but half way up the short hill Mike suddenly began to slow and then a tirade of swearing indicated he had got a puncture. His front wheel had dropped into a rut a few yards back and had caused a pinch puncture. The tyre went down rapidly. It was our first puncture and was fortunately to be our last. The tube was quickly replaced before we cycled on.

A short while later we stopped at Ancre Cemetery, its red brick walls towering over the road on our right. A van was parked on the gravel outside the cemetery, the logo of the Commonwealth War Graves Commission emblazoned on its sides. Three workmen were busy amongst the rows of gravestones, one was cleaning the headstones, another mowed the grass and the third was weeding the flowers beds that ran in front of the headstones. All the cemeteries in the care of the Commonwealth War Graves Commission are meticulously maintained. The headstones are cleaned and the carvings renewed when necessary to ensure that, as the dedication found at each cemetery declares, 'their name liveth forevermore'.

The Ancre Cemetery contains over 2500 graves, less than 1200 of which are identified. Most of the soldiers who are buried here took part in The Somme offensive in 1916 and in later fighting here in the Ancre valley in 1917. In spring of that year the German Army retreated from the area, enabling the Allies to clear the nearby battlefields of the dead and of make-shift graves, and to inter the remains here. Over one fifth of the men buried here were men of the 63rd (Royal Naval) Division who lost their lives over just three days of fighting in November 1916; a further 700 more from that Division have no known grave and their names appear on the nearby Thiepval Memorial visible on the wooded hillside in the distance.

We climbed a gradual hill, surrounded by woodland, from which the rippling laughing call of a green woodpecker rang out. To our left we could occasionally see the red and white bricks and stones of Thiepval Monument. At the top the trees thinned out and the view of Albert opened up ahead. We were looking across a landscape of arable fields and hedgerows to the two towers of the churches in Albert, one tower topped with a golden spire that caught the light as the sun emerged briefly from behind dark clouds.

Albert has a delightful centre, a pleasant square with a fountain and flower beds that is surrounded by shops and pavement cafes. With his back to the church, is the statue of a Scottish soldier playing the bagpipes, his bronze kilt blowing in the imaginary breeze. Scottish regiments lost many men to the fighting in this area. Albert is now a small, pleasant town but at the beginning of the war it had been occupied by the German Army, they did not stay long before retreating to the Marne following heavy bombardment by the Allies. No doubt the citizens breathed a collective sigh of relief at that point. Their relief was to be short lived though as with the Battle of the Somme in 1916 Albert became an important hub for the Allied Army. Albert was comprehensively flattened and finally rebuilt in the Art Deco style which is reflected in the shop fronts surrounding the square. One building that was faithfully rebuilt in the style of the original is the Basilica Notre Dame de Brebieres. Originally designed by the architect Edmond Duhoit it was only built between 1885 and 1897 and is certainly a grand and impressive building. But the original had barely twenty years of peace before the bombing of Albert started and in January 1915 a German shell hit the top of the steeple. Miraculously the steeple remained relatively intact but the statue of Mary and Baby Jesus began to lean until it was perched horizontally atop the spire. A legend soon arose that when the Leaning Virgin fell the war would end. Well, both were inevitable, the Virgin did fall in the spring of 1918 when the British Army shelled the now German-held Albert, deliberately targeting the steeple to prevent its use as an observation point.

To the side of the Basilica is the entrance to the Somme Museum. When we arrived there was an hour and a half remaining until it closed. Would this give us enough time to look at all the exhibits? We deliberated but not for long. Parked next to the entrance was a large coach, a familiar large coach. The school group we had encountered the day before were obviously inside the museum. We decided to delay our visit until the next day. Instead we cycled along the main road, took a couple of turnings and soon found a large supermarket. Leaving our bikes secured in the bike shelter I took advantage of a bin, oddly mounted at head height, to get rid of our litter from lunch time. I chucked the rubbish into the bin. It promptly landed at my feet. Faulty aim? No, faulty bin, there was no bottom in it. The rubbish went back in the pannier until I could find a better bin.

The car park was hot but the inside of the supermarket was air conditioned and the setting had clearly been programmed to Antarctic and we soon began to shiver. Another off-putting feature of this French shop was the smell that greeted us as soon as we entered. Ripe, festering cheese. Go in a British supermarket and I'm sure they feed the air con unit around the store via the bakery section because you always seem to be tempted by the smell of freshly baking bread. The French nose must be programmed to overspend on the essence of excessively ripe cheese. I can't say as I was tempted! Mike however seemed to be more appreciative.

"We could get some of that nice soft cheese we've had before," he enthused.

"Well, you could. I might stick to some chorizo."

"Ham?" he asked as we made our way through the deli section.

Call me fussy, call me English, call me insular and set in my ways, but wizened ham that resembles a dried up scab (not dissimilar to my arm come to think of it) and with a small swarm of flies settling on it doesn't really do it for me. The ham and the smelly cheese reminded me of an unsettling incident that had occurred the previous summer when we had been camping in France. We had bought a packet of ham which we had used over a few days to make sandwiches. On the third day as I opened the ham I was a bit puzzled to notice it was breaded ham.

"I don't remember buying breaded ham," I mused.

"Oh, I don't know what we got," replied Mike, which is no surprise as he eats so quickly he barely registers what he's consuming.

And on closer inspection the bread crumbs looked a bit odd. You tend not to get regular oval-shaped bread crumbs. That's when I realised I wasn't getting confused, we really hadn't bought breaded ham, it wasn't breadcrumbs lining the edge of the ham slices, it was flies' eggs! The rest of the ham went in Mike's sandwiches and I said nothing more. Just kidding. The ham went in the bin and we had cheese that day instead. A couple of days later, sitting atop a mountain and just finishing a packed lunch of cheese salad sandwiches, I noticed a small maggot in the bottom of the lunch box. Had that fallen in off an overhanging tree? Bit difficult, there were no trees this far up the mountain. Had it been hiding in the salad? I tried not to think about the possibility of other maggots that I had just eaten along with the sandwich. Maybe it was a one off! There were a lot of creepy crawlies about and inevitably some were getting into the tent. When we returned to the camp later that day the first thing I did was inspect the cheese. The lunch time visitor to the lunch box had not been a one off. Somehow the resident French flies had managed to invade the cool box, work their way into the packet of cheese and lay lots of eggs which had since hatched into lots of tiny white, cheese-coloured maggots. How had I not noticed when I had made the packed lunch that morning? I could only put it down to the maggots all hatching in unison during the day. The remaining cheese found itself in the same bin as the ham. And my sandwiches in future consisted of fillings that came out of screw top jars. Note to self: chocolate nut spread, jam and peanut butter make the best sandwiches! Being much more selective in my sandwich fillings I eventually put the insectivorous diet incident to the back of my mind. But an exhilarating downhill descent on the bikes a couple of days later, whizzing at speed with, apparently, my mouth unfortunately open, resulted in me swallowing a fly. By the end of the week I think I had ingested every stage of a fly's life cycle. As holiday gourmet food experiences go I have to say the American diet when we visited Yosemite was much more enjoyable than that French one had been. But like I said, call me fussy!

My friend and walking partner, Chris, had once eaten a chocolate covered cricket when offered one at a science conference we had attended.

"What did you do that for?" I had asked in amazement.

"I thought you were going to have one as well!" came her sheepish reply.

"You must be joking! What a waste of chocolate."

We browsed the supermarket for our by now usual picnic style evening meal of crusty fresh baguettes, salad, cheese ("not that stinky one!"), tart au citroen and fruit. Another bar of chocolate, this time with almond praline filling, and a couple of bottles of beer also managed to appear in the basket. The beer seemed rather appropriate for Mike, the picture on the bottle showed a bearded gnome on a unicycle. You can draw your own conclusions from that.

We crammed the shopping into the panniers. The baguette looked a bit precarious sticking out of the top so in the end I snapped it in half. And then we set off to find the accommodation for the next two nights. By chance we stumbled onto the Remembrance Cycle Route which led us out of Albert following a picturesque path beside a stream, through parkland and past several lakes into the nearby village of Aveluy. The stream was muddy with the recent rains and lapping at the top of the banks, and willows hung their branches close to the surface of the water. The grey brown water was not putting the ducks off and a mallard and her family of ducklings dabbled for food in the murky water.

"This is a nice route you've found us," I remarked.

"Ah! It is," he replied. "However, I programmed the sat nav on the car mode!"

"But we're in a park! So it's picked out a route you'd never get a car down!" I laughed.

We left the park through a narrow gate just wide enough for a bicycle or a pushchair, definitely not a car, and joined a quiet road past a couple of allotments and fields before reaching the centre of the village. We were booked into a wooden chalet in the grounds of a small house for the next two nights, which would give us time to explore the area close to The Somme battlefields. A note on the front door of the house greeted us, stating the owner would be returning from work at 6 p.m. and would come to meet us then. In the meantime, the note said, we should go through the gate on our left and into the garden to our chalet.

Mike opened the narrow double gate, a rickety thing of white painted metal. He wheeled his bike through and I followed but I when I attempted to close the gate I could not get the latch to engage with the lip on the other gate, one gate seemed to have dropped a bit. Leaning the bike against my hip I tried lifting one of the gates slightly. Success! I engaged the latch. Just one problem: I'd lifted one half of the gate off its hinges. The bike was beginning to topple, the gate was refusing to fit back onto its hinge pin. One handed with a useless immovable shoulder I was in danger of dropping both the gate and the bike.

"Mike!" I called.

"What?" came his muffled response from somewhere in the back garden.

"Help!"

"What have you done?" he asked with mock exasperation as he hurried back to find me balancing a bike and a gate against my hips.

"Nothing! I was trying to latch it but the hinge must have dropped on one side and now it's come off completely."

Mike took the gate out of my hand and quickly remounted it on the hinge pin before attempting to latch it.

"What have you done to it?" he muttered as he began to realise the gate was at fault and not me.

"See! It's not just me being my usual clumsy self."

A bit more muttering followed before he finally fixed the gate. I always say it's useful to go on holiday with a builder. He led the way into the garden.

"There's just one problem," he remarked.

"What's that?" I asked, hoping there were no more gates.

"We are only here for two nights!" he laughed.

As I emerged from the end of the path and into the garden I could see exactly what he meant. Our chalet was a quaint wooden cabin with a small veranda, upon which sat a picnic table and chairs.

Shade was provided by a sweet chestnut tree and nearby on the grassy lawn sat two sun loungers. The whole area was screened by hedges and close to the door of the chalet was a beautiful scented scarlet rose bush. Inside, the chalet was equally delightful with a small kitchen and dining table, two comfy armchairs and against the back wall a large double bed, leading off to the right at the rear of the chalet was a small en suite shower room.

"Put the kettle on!" I grinned, unpacking the food and our supply of English tea bags.

Tea bags, biscuits, coffee, sugar and milk were already provided but after the disappointing tea at breakfast that morning I stuck to the English teabags, the French biscuits were very good though. On the small dining table were another welcome note and a handful of sweets in cellophane wrappers. But we were not the first to find the sweets! Across the table marched a line of minute ants, all were heading for the sweets and some had already managed to find their way into the wrappers. I followed the line back, across the table cloth, over the edge and onto the wall where a corner of the cloth touched the wood, then up the wall to the bottom of the window frame. Removing the sweets I took the table cloth outside and gave it a shake over the rose bush, then moved the table away from the wall before covering it with the cloth once more. The ants might only have been tiny but they were persistent and over the next couple of days the table cloth would be shaken out several times and the table gradually moved further and further away from the wall. Fortunately the ants were easy to remove and never ventured further than the dining table.

We took our tea and beer and slumped wearily in the sun loungers, relaxing and enjoying the late afternoon sunshine. A second beer appeared along with a packet of crisps. When did he sneak those into the shopping basket? As Mike belched quietly and muttered something about gassy Belgian beer a blackbird and a robin sang from the hedgerows and sparrows flittered about the garden and those on either side. Newly fledged sparrows sat on a branch, cheeping and flapping their little wings, beaks gaping as their parents flew in to feed them insects.

Seeing something else being fed reminded me how hungry I was myself and with my cup empty I went inside to put the kettle on again and to have a shower. Mike followed suit and soon we were showered and dressed, not without a battle on my part to pull a T-shirt over my head one handed. ("Do you want some help?" "Yes please. Ouch!" "Sorry.")

We took our picnic tea out onto the patio, making rather a mess with the crispy baguettes which we seemed to be sharing not just with the sparrows but with another line of those minute ants. After our meal we set off to stroll back down the lane to the lakes we had cycled past earlier. As the sun was beginning to sink we watched fishermen on the lakes, a line of joggers and some children on bicycles all making the most of the pleasant spring evening. A chiff chaff called from a willow tree, young moorhens squeaked in the reeds at the edge of the pond and three grebes glided gracefully over the still waters of the lake.

When we got back to the chalet I had yet more trouble with the gates again.

"Help!"

"You're not fit to be let out!" sighed Mike rolling his eyes.

Wednesday 30th May 2018. 43 miles.

The owner of the chalet, a friendly local who spoke excellent English, brought us a breakfast basket early the next morning. She had arrived home from work the previous evening as we had been relaxing on the loungers and after chatting for a little while about our cycle ride and the battlefields (it transpired she worked in the local tourist office and often acted as group leader on guided battlefield walks) she had confirmed what time we would like breakfast. The basket was full of croissants, yoghurt, bottles of fresh local apple juice, fruit and a crusty French stick with pots of jam and butter. We shared breakfast with the ants before packing up the remains for lunch, negotiating the gates and cycling off on a circular tour of that part of The Somme battlefields.

At the beginning of 1916 the German Army under command of General Falkenhayn mounted a massive attack at Verdun. Their aim was to crush the French Army which had already suffered heavy losses in the first two years. Heroically the French Army held, slowing the German advance until it was halted in March. Desperate for respite the French Army urged the British to help relieve pressure on the French and so Britain attacked German lines on The Somme in July. But the German position on The Somme had changed little in two years; two years in which the Imperial German Army had had plenty of time to fortify their position. The Germans were secure in their two lines of well dug trenches, backed up by communication trenches, and fronted by defensive lines of barbed wire which, according to one British machine gunner, were so thick that it was almost impossible to see through. Concrete dugouts had been built deep below the surface, these were to prove vital in protecting German soldiers from the heavy opening bombardment to come. Machine gun posts, constructed in concrete, were located in strategic positions from which interlocking areas of fire would cut down any attacking enemy soldiers.

Preparations for the Battle of The Somme had been meticulous. And it is a bitter irony that after two months of planning and countless drills the attack failed within the first few minutes. Moves were practised over replica trenches for weeks leading up to the assault, and then the movement of supplies and kit were practised. To the men it must have seemed like they could not fail.

But the Germans were not fools. Their spotter planes had taken photos of the fake German trenches and if that was not enough the Germans could not fail to notice the new trenches being dug connecting trenches that stretched out into no-man's-land. Forewarned by all this the Germans planned accordingly. But this in a way had been part of the Allied plan!

The objective of The Somme offensive was not so much to gain ground as to relieve pressure at Verdun – the Allies wanted the Germans to send more troops to The Somme, thus taking them away from Verdun. Inflicting heavy losses on the German Army was seen as a secondary objective. As history was to prove these objectives were not met and it was the Allies that were to suffer the heaviest losses. A week of heavy artillery bombardment preceded the attack, during which some 1.7 million shells were fired by the British Army. Pauses in the bombardment were intended to fool the Germans into emerging and exposing their concealed batteries. They were not fooled. Bad weather then saw the attack date put back by two days and the bombardment extended and tens of thousands of wet, muddy, frightened, tired men were left waiting.

The commanding officers, the high command, of the Great War have earned a reputation for their reckless decisions, costly plans, for hiding miles behind the front lines ensconced in luxury in their requisitioned villas and chateaux. Much of this reputation is deserved, perhaps not all, but many of their orders can only leave questions of why and for what purpose those decisions were made. Not least the decision made by General Snow, Company Commander of the 46th Division.

For two brigades of this Division, the ill-fated Staffordshires and Sherwood Foresters, the protracted two days of waiting was to be made even worse. For in his infinite stupidity General Snow decided he would like to see his men practise one last time. So they were marched back ten miles just to entertain General Snow, and then they were marched the ten miles back to the front. They must have been exhausted. Less than twelve hours after returning to the front many of them were dead, wounded or missing: trapped on the barbed wire that the barrage had failed to clear or mown down by machine gun fire, or cut down by the enfilade fire from the German defences on 'The Z' a spur of the German front line that had also not been wiped out by British heavy artillery bombardment.

Eventually the weather improved, the waiting was over. And on 1st July 1916 from 7.20 a.m. until 7.30 mines were detonated under the German trenches. At 7.30 whistles blew along the front line and men climbed over the top and walked into no-man's-land. They had been instructed to advance at a walking pace to maintain an orderly attack. They had been told the wire would have been destroyed and the German soldiers killed by the bombardment. They advanced at two miles an hour, as if they were taking a Sunday afternoon stroll. One Battalion even kicked a football as they went, a ploy their commanding officer had thought up with a reward for the first of his men to get the ball into the enemy trenches. But the bombardment had not destroyed the German trenches or the machine gun posts or the heavy artillery. The German soldiers manned the Maxim guns and the heavy artillery, the infantry took up their rifles, and the British and French Armies were mown down and blown to pieces. At Gommecourt Wood as the smoke from the British artillery cleared the Sherwood Foresters were exposed and the Germans emerged from behind them to slaughter them.

The bombardment from the British heavy artillery failed for several reasons. Some shells missed their targets – there was a shortage of experienced bombardiers and so the range finding was inaccurate. The planned protective creeping barrage during the advance did not materialise – again due to the lack of experienced bombardiers. Many of the shells were duds – it has been estimated that up to one third did not detonate. The wrong type of shell was used – only high explosive artillery was effective at destroying deep trenches and the British Army had insufficient supplies of this type of ordnance. Furthermore the soft chalk of the terrain acted as a cushion for the explosive impact of the shells.

Delays in communication only served to worsen the situation on The Somme. Once things began to go wrong in the advance it took four hours to organise another bombardment. The troops were doomed before they ever went over the top. The trenches were filled with mud turned red with blood by the end of the first day. To quote Captain John Milne of the Leicestershire Regiment 'the taps of The Somme bloodbath are full on.'

On the 3rd July The Times newspaper published the following report on the Battle: "Everything has gone well. Our troops have successfully carried out their missions, all counter-attacks have been repulsed and large number of prisoners taken." As a piece of fake news it would be hard to find a better example in all the First World War reporting. The truth was far different.

Approximately 100,000 British soldiers went over the top on the opening day of the Battle of the Somme. Over half would become casualties and nearly one in five would be killed; the figures are staggering: 57,470 were injured, and of these 19,240 were killed. Most of these died within the first hour of battle. The German soldiers had been trained to identify British officers and on the first day alone 60% were killed. The first day of the Battle of The Somme was, and still is, the British Army's greatest loss in a single day.

I find it difficult to imagine what this number of men would look like. It is such a large figure that in a way it becomes yet another shocking but inconceivable statistic. So in an effort to gain some sort of perspective I found myself searching the internet for seating capacity at sporting venues and for towns in Britain with similar populations. Over 57,000 casualties on the first day of the Somme would more than fill the 55,000 seater Etihad Stadium, home to Manchester City Football Club; it would not quite fill the 60,000 seater stadium at Celtic Park, and there would have been some empty seats in the 80,000 seater 2012 London Olympic Stadium. This number of casualties is roughly the same as the populations, according to the 2011 census, of Macclesfield or Aldershot; whilst smaller towns such as Dorchester, Stowmarket and Ely would have been completely wiped out.

The Pals Battalions were especially badly affected on the first day of The Somme and the battle was to mark the end of Kitchener's Pals Battalions. The famous Accrington Pals formed one division of the 11th Service Battalion of the East Lancashire Regiment. The Accrington Pals also included the Pals from Burnley, Chorley and Blackburn. Two of my great uncles were in the Burnley Pals. On their way to the front line the Accrington Pals passed the Royal Army Medical Corps Advanced Dressing Station at Basin Wood. Adjacent to the dressing station a mass grave had already been dug, they could see it as they marched past. Many of these men from the mill towns of East Lancashire would be returned to it.

On the first day of the Battle of the Somme the East Lancashire Regiment attacked the village of Serre-les-Puisieux. There were approximately 700 men of the Accrington Pals in action. In the first half hour of battle 235 were killed and 350 wounded. The Accrington Pals were virtually wiped out. It is said that there was not a street in the little industrial mill town that was not in mourning for one or more of its men. Thirty of these dead men were from Burnley. The corpses remained tangled in the wire in no-man's-land in front of Serre until February 1916 when the Germans withdrew to new positions. By that time there was little left to bury or to help identify them.

East Lancashire was, of course, not the only county suffering huge losses that day. The men of the 8th and 9th Devonshires are buried in the trench they set out from and a memorial remembers their sacrifice: "The Devonshires held this trench; the Devonshires hold it still." The original memorial had been a simple carved wooden cross but this went missing and it was not replaced until the 1980s, when a group of British soldiers and officers, some of whom were Devonshires, led by Lieutenant Colonel Graham Parker were on a tour of The Somme battlefields. Learning of the missing memorial they decide to raise money to replace the cross. The result is a stone memorial that stands at the entrance to the cemetery; it bears the same inscription as the humble wooden cross.

The Battle of The Somme staggered bloodily on through the summer and autumn of 1916. On 15th September, on a section of front running for ten miles between Combles and the Ancre valley, tanks were used for the first time but with limited success. Of the three dozen or so that set out many were incapacitated or became stuck. By October the weather was working against the troops, intense and prolonged rain turned already damaged country lanes and tracks into impassable quagmires. Shell holes became flooded bogs, anything, man or horse, that fell into them often drowned. It made the transportation of men, supplies, food and ammunition difficult at best and impossible at worst. One historical account described the scene as a 'wilderness of mud' and likened the conditions in which the infantry soldiers found themselves as 'to those of earthworms'.

By mid-November the dreadful weather put an end to further fighting on The Somme for that year. In just over four months an average of five miles of Allied advance had been achieved along the fourteen mile section of the front. Casualty numbers were staggering: British 419,654; French 204,253; German somewhere between 465,000 and 680,000. It is often quoted that for every 100 yards of advance 1000 Allied lives were lost.

Our ride that day was a 43 mile circular and we left Aveluy heading roughly north to the Thiepval Memorial. We followed quiet lanes passing small woodlands that would have been obliterated a century ago. As the road began to climb along the hillside we could see the towering walls of the memorial across the swaying fields of wheat. We reached the small village and cycled round to the rear of the monument, leaving the bikes propped against a hedge we walked out to the memorial along a neat gravel path. Atop the monument the Union Jack and the Tricolor flew above this the largest of all the First World War memorials to the missing. Below on the grassy sward rows of the by now familiar British and Commonwealth headstones, 300 in all, were set out in neat lines on the right, whilst on the left were the simpler crosses of French soldiers' graves, again 300 in number; comrades in death, as one inscription read.

Thiepval Monument is visible for miles across the surrounding countryside, standing atop this once strategically important ridge, a ridge that had been so important to both sides during the conflict. As we walked through the monument we could appreciate just how large it is but the design for the original had been even larger. The sheer size had dictated the need for deep foundations but as construction began in 1929 it soon became clear the engineers were excavating through the remains of German trenches, uncovering the remains of soldiers and a quantity of unexploded ordnance in the process. By 1932 the memorial was completed and stood in a landscape still bereft of trees. Today majestic beech trees flank the memorial, the fields have been smoothed flat and the village has been rebuilt.

We walked under and around the soaring arches, each wall covered with carved panels listing the Regiments and the names of the missing from those regiments. Over 73,000 missing men. In 1932 the Thiepval Memorial was officially inaugurated, its architect Sir Edwin Lutyens attended as did the President of France, the Prince of Wales and veterans of the conflict amongst others.

On the bottoms of some of the panels were addendums where names of the missing had been added later. How had the authorities not realised sooner that these men were missing? Why had they been added afterwards?

"Perhaps they were the soldiers cleaning up the battlefields, recovering bodies later on, who were killed by unexploded shells," Mike pondered. "Or perhaps they died later of wounds."

"They'd hardly be missing though would they if they'd died of wounds?"

"Oh yeah! Fair point."

It was sadly telling of the numbers killed in the First World War that we never cycled more than a couple of miles before seeing another road sign pointing to another military cemetery. At the small crossroad at Thiepval signs pointed in various directions to other cemeteries and monuments. We headed next for the Ulster Tower cycling past fields laden with scarlet poppies. The tower was set back from the road in a walled, landscaped area of neatly mown grass with an avenue of small trimmed fir trees flanking the drive to the tower. The tower is an eye catching sight, not in keeping with the French countryside surrounding it, it is a replica of Helen's Tower from an estate in County Down in Ireland. On this site on 1st July 1916 men of the 36th Ulster Division went over the top to advance on the German lines. It was another tragic piece of the bloody tapestry of the first day of the Somme. The regiment won nine Victoria Crosses that day at a cost of over 5000 casualties. Only four of every five men who set out returned, the others were either killed, injured, taken prisoner or missing in action.

As we were leaving the grounds a minibus appeared from the museum behind the tower and I stopped to hold the gate open so he could drive out. As he drew level the man wound down the window and thanked me.

"You're the first person who's done that," he remarked in an Irish accent.

I was surprised to hear him say that as it seemed such an obvious thing to do. I was also surprised to hear his accent. But as we were to later discover nationals from the various countries often work in this area at the monuments and museums dedicated to their particular country's soldiers.

We cycled on, past large fields of wheat and sugar beet. Dosed up on ibuprofen I was feeling slightly better, the range of movement in my shoulder was beginning to increase and I tentatively tried changing gear with my left hand. The day before it had been too painful even to flick the gear lever on the drop handle bars but that morning I was able to do it with hardly any pain. By the end of the week I'd be doing cartwheels. Well, maybe not, unless I came off again!

The heavy rains of two days ago had washed much of the light brown soil onto the roads where it had quickly dried into lumps and dust, making for uncomfortable cycling as we tried to swerve the bumps or had to cycle over them. Cresting the ridge we headed towards the village of Pozieres sitting either side of the old Roman road. Australian soldiers had been stationed here during the Battle of the Somme. Old photographs from that time show a bleak landscape, the village had been completely obliterated by the bombardment; the landscape smashed beyond recognition. On the many information boards dotted around the reconstructed village we read of the efforts of the Australians and looked at photographs showing the surviving troops sheltering and exhausted after taking the ridge.

A short cycle ride along this former Roman road we came to The Windmill, little more than a bump in the ground now where the windmill had once stood. Behind it was the memorial to the nine million animals – regimental mascots, carrier pigeons, horses, mules, dogs – that were used and died during the First World War. There are three other memorials close by. The Australian Memorial commemorates the 2nd Division who lost so many men here, and another to the 1st Division. Across the road is the Tank Corps Memorial which commemorates the first time tanks were used in battle at Flers-Courcelette in September 1916. In front of this is a sculpture of a model tank.

From here we cycled back to Pozieres, leaving the bikes to look around the remains of the trenches and to read the inscriptions on yet another memorial. When the Australian forces took Pozieres in 1916 they must have hoped it would remain in Allied hands, but this was not the case. And as so often happened during this bloody war of attrition and of repeated advance and retreat the Germans would later retake the area. On the walls of the grandly colonnaded Pozieres Memorial lists the names of nearly 15,000 South African and British troops with no known graves, these men died fighting the Second Battle of the Somme in the spring and summer of 1918. Inside the large walled enclosure lie hundreds more men who died in the battle.

Pozieres was another reminder of all the hundreds of thousands of soldiers who had come from Commonwealth countries to fight for Britain during the war. Just a week before this cycling holiday I had been on a field trip with the college where I work and was sitting in a youth hostel in Snowdonia talking to another guest, a lady from Australia. She had seen me reading one of the travel guide books to the First World War and a lengthy chat ensued about her own visit to the Western Front in search of a great uncle.

"I made my son stand by his gravestone as I took a photograph," she told me, finishing with moist eyes, "then I realised my son was the age my great uncle had been when he died."

When she asked how we were travelling and I told her by bike she enthused that it was the best way to see the Western Front.

"It's huge! There's so much to see, cycling put the landscape into perspective."

She went on to tell me that proportionally Australia sacrificed more men than any other nation. She was proud and saddened in equal measure.

We left Pozieres following a quiet road turning off the main road to the left and quickly reached perhaps the most well-known crater of all: Lochnagar Crater. We locked the bikes to a fence close to the cross and its skirt of poppy wreaths and followed the duckboards around the perimeter, reading the many information boards as we went. Skylarks sang constantly overhead as they had sung over the battlefields a century ago. In the near distance, rising above the sloping fields, the gold statue atop the church at Albert could be seen.

Lochnagar Crater is perhaps the most infamous of the mine craters. It was created on the first day of the Battle of the Somme, 1st July 1916. The Royal Engineers had specialist Tunnelling Companies, often made up of many British miners, volunteers who had left their homes and families, abandoning the dangers of the coalface for the other even more perilous dangers. These former miners toiled beneath Flanders digging tunnels and shafts under the German lines, not just here but on other parts of the Western Front. At Lochnagar in order to create the chamber to hold the explosives engineers sank a shaft 120 metres (some 400 feet) and then tunnelled an inclined shaft towards the German front line, stopping 30 metres before it at a depth of 15 metres (50 feet). The tunnels measured 4.5 feet high by 2.5 feet wide, and in a day approximately 17 feet of tunnel would be excavated using just picks and shovels. The Germans were digging their own shafts and the need for silence became increasingly important the closer the men of the 179th

Tunnelling Company came to the German front line. As a result progress became painfully slow with the men using their bayonets to prise loose flints whilst another tunneller waited to catch the rock as it fell.

At the time the detonation was believed to be the largest man-made explosion and it was heard as far away as England. The crater formed when the explosives were detonated is approximately 70 feet deep and 300 feet in diameter. A size that is difficult to comprehend just from a description alone. Dozens and dozens of German soldiers were killed and the site is now classed as a war grave. But until 1978 Lochnagar was being treated with anything but respect as a war grave. The local landowner had neglected the crater and it was being used as a rubbish dump and by motocross riders. The crater was saved by British man, Richard Dunning MBE, who bought the crater, cleaned it out and preserved the heritage, the history. Lochnagar is now a memorial to all those who lost their lives in the Great War. Today it is carefully preserved and relies heavily on donations to keep the site maintained. Schools are encouraged to sponsor plaques, which are set into the duckboards, and many of these plaques commemorate former pupils or regiments with a close affiliation with the school.

The Battle of The Somme was a tragedy of unbelievable scale. But inevitably there were immense acts of bravery and self-sacrifice. Leading his men of the 24th Battalion of the Northumberland Fusiliers over the top on the first day of the battle, Lieutenant Colonel Louis Meredith Howard was seriously wounded and trapped on the German wire. He was rescued by one of his men, Bombing Sergeant Patrick Butler, who risked his own life crawling out across the battlefield to bring back his commanding officer. The men sheltered in Lochnagar Crater. But they were still far from safe and tragically Sergeant Butler was killed by a sniper's bullet whilst looking after his commanding officer. The next day Lieutenant Colonel Howard died of his wounds. The men were buried in Ovillers Military Cemetery and every year on 1st July at the Lochnagar Remembrance Ceremony two wreaths are laid to honour their memory.

As we sat on the grass eating lunch a male blackbird flew up onto the top of the cross and began singing. His melodic song competing with the rising and falling song of a skylark. It was the hottest day so far and other people coming to visit the crater looked sunburnt and exhausted as they wandered the site and read the plaques as we had done. A group of motorcyclists drew up, their engines roaring noisily, breaking the quiet atmosphere. The leather-clad bikers with their tattoos and beer bellies walked round the site as reverently as the rest. Two motor homes arrived next, disgorging baby boomer pensioners. Then a minibus of teenagers from a school in Kent. Everyone seemed affected by this immense crater, it illustrated the destructive power of the battles far more than the preserved trenches at Bayernwald or the grassed over mounds of half-filled shell holes at Hill 60.

Quiet lanes and small villages marked our route that afternoon. Wheat fields stretched across the gently rolling landscape and in one place two fields of red poppies stood out against the patchwork of green. We passed through the sleepy village of Frise, heading up a gradual slope to the viewpoint above the Somme Valley, where the remains of German trenches looked out over the meandering waterways, canal, lush copses and green fields. The undulating chalk hillside, dotted with craters and the vague indents where lines of trenches had once stood, was now a nature reserve rich with rare lime loving plants and orchids where every footstep disturbed clouds of blue butterflies.

Quaint French villages, quiet sunny lanes, the smell of cut grass and flowers marked our ride to the village of Bray sur Somme. It all seemed very continental, very French and then…

"It's left here!" came a Scottish voice.

A cyclist had just appeared over the brow of the hill and stopped on the other side of the road from where we had stopped at a junction with a main road leading towards Albert. Mike was consulting his phone's sat nav once again, peering over the top of his varifocals in a myopic manner and muttering to it.

"Bonjour!" called the Scot.

"Hiya!" I replied.

"Parlez vous Anglais?"

"Well I am English," I laughed.

"Ach, you probably speak it pretty well then," he replied.

"Oh, I don't know about that!"

At that point he was joined by two other cyclists whereupon we all had a chat, shouting across the road about our routes, where we had cycled from and where we were cycling to. The group of three had caught the same ferry as us but then a train to Arras and were planning to cycle to Verdun further down the Western Front. Wishing each other safe rides we parted company, with Mike and me cycling up the long hill to return to Albert. We followed a main road with the surroundings gradually becoming more industrial. In the distance was the shining golden statue atop the church in Albert but dominating the foreground was a vast aerospace factory with the nose of A380 parked outside. As we were descending towards the factory Mike's chain came off. Whilst Mike got his hands mucky putting it back on I started looking at the flowering plants in the roadside verge.

"I'm glad your chain chose this point to come off," I remarked, fumbling to get my camera out of the pannier.

"Why?" he grunted.

"Because there's a bee orchid here, look."

This rare and delicate orchid, so named because it resembles a bumble bee's bottom sticking out of a flower, was the first such orchid I had seen. For this holiday at least it would also be the last.

With the chain back where it was supposed to be we cycled down the hill, joining a cycle path along the pavement that obviously served the workers at the aerospace factory and the other units along the road into Albert. As we reached the centre of the town we diverted down a busy shopping street, stopping at a pharmacy to buy some more ibuprofen for my shoulder.

Leaving Mike happily guarding the bikes, I say happily as the neighbouring shop to the pharmacist was a lingerie boutique, I went inside the chemist's shop. An elderly lady was waiting while one assistant bagged up her purchases. The other assistant was deep in conversation with a young mum who, toddler astride her right hip, seemed to be describing some horrendously contagious childhood pox in graphic detail. The young woman behind the counter was nodding, serious expression welded to her face and every so often would issue a shrug or a tut before proffering one remedy or another. Meanwhile the sickly infant snotted and drooled over the foot of a plastic troll and most of his mother's arm. I began searching the shelves for analgesics but could only find a selection of cough remedies, indigestion remedies and toothpaste. The painkillers, when I finally did spot them, were lurking out of reach behind the counter. Unlike in Britain, French supermarkets are not allowed to sell painkillers, only pharmacists have that prerogative. The recently elected President of France had tentatively proposed this law should be relaxed to allow supermarkets and other outlets to begin selling them. However, this proposal was met with strong opposition from the pharmacists of France, strikes were threatened and the idea was quietly shelved. Eventually the young woman and her contagious child left the shop, tracking a snail trail of slime in their wake.

"Bonjour," the assistant said turning to me.

"Er, bonjour," I hesitantly replied. I could see what I wanted, would it be easier to just point to it and look an idiot or should I try a bit of French and come across as an even bigger idiot? I opted for the politer option. "Parlez vous Anglais?"

"Ooh, a little."

"Er, ibuprofen s'il vous plait?"

"Ah, oui!" she responded, and reached down a packet of ibuprofen.

"Deux, s'il vous plait," I attempted.

So far so good, she reached for a second packet and began to ring up the purchases. Two packets of a generic brand of ibuprofen at home would probably cost 60p, the cost in France was over five Euros! No wonder the French pharmacists were keen to keep their monopoly on painkillers.

"You must only take one," she cautioned.

One! For that price I was going to finish the packet.

"They are tres strong, yes?" she added.

"Ah! Oui! Yes! One, yes," I replied.   Double strength and twice the size, at least I didn't have issues swallowing tablets.

Feeling rather pleased at having purchased something without too much difficulty or embarrassment I returned to Mike who seemed particularly taken with a voluptuous life sized plastic mannequin, although not everything about it was life sized, some things were more than life sized.

"Like that yellow and blue string bikini, do you?" I asked sneaking up behind him.

"Uh! No, I was looking at the scenery backdrop, wondering where it was..." he mumbled.

"With your navigating I've been doing that most of this week!"

We wheeled the bikes down to the square in front of the basilica and crossed the road to the Somme 1916 Museum, located in the underground passages that can be accessed by the side of the basilica. We paid a paltry sum, received a pair of 3D spectacles and a mock identity card for a genuine member of the Allied Armies and were directed down a flight of steps into the tunnels. At the bottom of the steps on the left was a small room where every fifteen minutes a 3D film played out of The Battle of the Somme, we sat watching that amongst a group of Dutch men. Then we made our way along the 250 metres of tunnels where display cases lined the walls. There were uniforms, weapons, personal items recovered from the battlefields, dioramas depicting bunkers and officers' quarters both German and Allied. Some display cases contained rusting relics of shells and grenades. Others contained letters home and diaries, boxes of rations, photographs. Perhaps the most disturbing display of all was the different kinds of explosive shells and grenades, some cut away to show their intricate working parts. The amount of time, thought and design that had been invested simply in order to create so many ways to maim and kill was horrifying. And along the walls were information boards detailing facts and figures, life stories of the combatants and accounts of battles and daily life in the trenches.

We emerged from the tunnels into daylight and a room with more information about the people whose identity cards we had been issued with at the entrance. Beyond that was a gift shop. The inevitable gift shop. The only exit from the museum was through the gift shop. Show me a museum or an attraction that doesn't have this same layout and I will be surprised. It is smart marketing to get the tourists to part with more money. But I do have issues with tourism rooted in the loss of millions of lives.

The First World War has spawned its own tourism. And it is a somewhat a ghoulish thought to have to acknowledge that people, businesses and tour companies make money and are in existence purely because war was waged here: men, boys, women, horses, mules and others died and suffered unimaginable horror here a century ago. But battlefield tourism is not a new thing and it could be argued that the British Government at the time of the First World War instigated it, even if unwittingly. By 1915 this Government had banned repatriation of the fallen, a policy that was to continue even after the war. So any relatives wishing to visit the graves of their loved ones had no choice but to travel to the Western Front to do so. Also by 1915 a 'tourist line' had been established near Ypres in what was then an area away from the main fighting where politicians, journalists and other noteworthy visitors could safely watch the conflict from a distance. Tour operator Thomas Cook had, until 1915, been running trips to the area and it was only due to the opposition of the French that these ceased. That highly respected publication, the Michelin Guide, had by 1917 published its first guide to the Western Front. It is hard to imagine anything comparable in modern times. Soldiers of the Great War themselves also indulged in a bit of sightseeing and the word souvenir only came into use in the English language following the war when returning British soldiers brought back mementoes from the battlefield. It was not uncommon for soldiers on both sides to take helmets, badges, buttons and other items as souvenirs from captured enemy trenches.

After the war the first 'tourists' to visit the Western Front were bereaved relatives. Later in the twentieth century as men who had fought in the war gradually began to retire they returned to honour their fallen comrades. In the early 1990s the new National Curriculum put the history of the First World War on the English school history syllabus and soon many schools were taking pupils on trips to the Western Front and the many cemeteries there. As the centenary of the war approached more people made the pilgrimage, many like us had family connections and felt a need to travel to the place where their ancestors had suffered so much.

So call it what you will: ghoulish sightseeing, curiosity, homage, pilgrimage, respectful search for answers and understanding. All the people we were to meet on our visit to the Western Front were there not for enjoyment but out of respect. And that can only be a good thing.

What I did struggle to justify and accept was the huge market in souvenirs of the Western Front that tourism has inevitably spawned. It was one thing for fighting men at the time to bring home souvenirs but for modern day visitors to the Front to have the opportunity to purchase souvenirs of their visit sits uneasily with me. We were to see many shops selling Great War themed beer, chocolate, pate, whisky to name but a few of the edible mementoes available. There are Menin Gate themed key rings and pens ad nauseam and of course everything and anything poppy. The money tourists bring to the economy via accommodation providers, museums and tours is one thing, but to me these tasteless souvenirs and the money they generate for the tat shops (and no doubt the manufacturers back in China) seems not merely disrespectful but obscene. Take one look at the ranks of gravestones in the dozens and dozens of military cemeteries, the list of the missing carved at the Menin Gate and other places and then ask yourself is it really fitting and respectful to buy a fridge magnet or a golden bullet key ring? Selling poppies and other items to raise money for worthy causes like the Royal British Legion and Help for Heroes is admirable and should be encouraged but I struggled to deal with the ethics of this blatant commercialism. Where was the integrity of the vendors and those who bought such items? When I had first proposed the idea of another book about our cycle ride along the Western Front Mike had been quick to question how I felt about profiting from any sales, small though these invariably are. He had vocalised concerns I had been feeling from the outset of the idea. The solution was simple: any profits from the sale of this book will be donated to the Royal British Legion and Help for Heroes.

So with my aversion to gift shops in general and First World War-reliant gift shops in particular I was especially offended by several glass cases of items for sale in the museum gift shop in Albert. For sums of money ranging from a few Euros to several hundred it was possible to purchase genuine items that had been used in the war. Vases that had been made from polished shell cases, buttons scavenged from tunics from the battlefields, personal items of long dead soldiers that had been found by dedicated treasure hunters who made a living from digging up and metal detecting along the Western Front. There were photographs, cutlery, shaving kits, helmets – some still bearing the marks of shrapnel, regimental badges that still had bits of thread attached where they had been sewn onto a uniform. Field glasses, mess tins, belt buckles, bibles, notebooks. The list of items that had been plundered from the earth, cleaned up and offered for sale as souvenirs to the public was long, varied and ghoulish. For some people the power of possession of these personal artefacts was fuelling a market that seem completely disrespectful to the men who fought. And I was reminded of the words of Wilfred Owen's poem, Dulce et Decorum Est, describing the eager proponents of the war as having 'such high zest' and of those eager hangers on (children) 'ardent for some desperate glory'. I could not understand the need to possess such items, particularly if they had no family connection to the buyer. A comparison would be going to Auschwitz and buying a shoe.

We emerged from the museum feeling informed but tainted by the blatant commercialism. It was a relief to emerge into the sunshine and birdsong and the scent of flowers in a small park with shrubs, a water feature and colourful flower beds.

"It's very nice out here," I remarked. "But where are we?"

The winding, protracted tunnels of the museum, which I had imagined to be looping round the Basilica had actually carried us under the square with its splashing fountain, under more side streets and shops and houses before spewing us out several hundred yards from where we had entered. Once out of the little park it was easy to see where we needed to go, or at least I thought so, Mike's inbuilt sense of direction however seemed to have gone haywire. It must be catching from his mobile's sat nav app.

"It's down here," I pointed, heading back towards the square.

"Are you sure?" he asked, spinning round and trying to get his bearings.

"Yep, come on! Trust me for once."

"Well, you usually get us lost..."

"Look! The Basicila is there! You can hardly miss it," I snapped with mock offense.

I didn't get us lost and we soon reached the square.

"Oh, we're here!" exclaimed Mike as if we had just travelled back from Narnia. "There're our bikes!"

"You don't need to sound so surprised," I sighed. "But you do need to navigate us to the nearest supermarket so we can get something for tea."

The supermarket, when we reached it, had sold out of religieuse. Mike's face dropped.

"You having a stroke?" I asked teasingly.

"No, but there're no religieuse."

"Okay, brace yourself – we might have to get a different sort of patisserie!"

Supplies of tarte au citroen had not run out. Thank goodness.

Back at the chalet we relaxed with beer (Mike), tea (me, er and Mike), crisps (mainly Mike and the ants). The crisps lived up to their name and very soon the ants were racing across the grass, having given up the tablecloth in favour of the more easily accessible crumb-covered ground around the sun loungers. We spent a pleasant evening of lounging around, eating another delicious cheese, ham, baguette and salad meal and generally being rather idle. Mike had his head firmly embedded in maps and I had mine firmly embedded in various packets of biscuits and chocolate. For much of the evening entertainment came in the form of a male house sparrow that was busily chasing flies around the garden, swooping and diving as he struggled to catch them.

Thursday 31th May. 25 miles.

The breakfast basket arrived that morning just as we were packing the panniers onto our bikes. The B&B owner stopped to chat and tell us arrangements for leaving the key when we left. Working at the tourist office in Albert had given her a great deal of knowledge about the war and the sights of interest in the area. She was interested to know where we were from and when Mike explained he lived in the Lake District she quickly told us she had been there on a visit to nearby Ulverston.

"Why Ulverston?" Mike asked.

"It is twinned with Albert! I went as part of a group from the town."

"Of course!" exclaimed Mike. "That's why the name Albert seems so familiar to me."

She asked our plans for the day and then wished us safe journey before hurrying off to work. A short time later we heard a faint metallic clatter. Half an hour later and wheeling our laden bikes down through the garden the source of the clatter became apparent. The metal gate was propped against the house wall, clean off its hinges.

"See!" I exclaimed indignantly. "I'm not the only one who has trouble with that gate!"

We were now on the return leg of our trip. Our destination that day would be Arras but our route on this return leg would take us to different parts of the Western Front. There was still much to see and we were already realising this single week would not be enough. At some point in the future we would return.

It was a cloudy start to the day, although that was not to last long and by the time we were cycling up the hill towards Beaumont-Hamel the sun was already beginning to break through. We left the bikes secured in the car park at one side of the road before crossing into the preserved battle ground and heading for the raised mound overlooking the site.

Beaumont-Hamel sat strategically above the Ancre Valley on the northern edge of the front where The Somme offensive was to take place. Held by the Germans it had been heavily fortified and was yet another target that the Allied Armies had set their sights on winning on 1st July 1916. Like other points along The Somme, mines had been laid here too but with typical mismanagement the one under Beaumont-Hamel detonated ten minutes too soon, forewarning the Germans of the imminent attack. As the men of the Newfoundland Regiment went over the top at 7.30 that morning the Germans were waiting for them. 780 Newfoundlanders set out, within half an hour only 110 were unscathed. It would be a further four and a half months before Beaumont-Hamel was eventually captured.

To honour their dead the Dominion of Newfoundland, a proudly separate part of Canada, purchased the land in the vicinity of the battle. The trenches and the shell-pocked area of no-man's-land are now preserved and various memorials and monuments are dotted around the site together with a visitor centre staffed by Newfoundlanders themselves. The field of battle is one of the best preserved of the many along the Western Front and the trenches, at times in close proximity to the German trenches, are accessible by a network of footpaths. It is possible to walk along some of the trenches, their bases protected by duckboards and the once sheer-sided sandbagged walls now sloping and grass-covered. The land is densely covered by shell holes, indication of the vast number of shells that were used during the battle. The best view of the site is from the small man-made mound on top of which sits a bronze caribou, the emblem of the Newfoundland Division. At the base of the mound is a memorial to the men of the Newfoundland Regiment. From atop the mound we could look down across the grass covered landscape towards Y Ravine, a deep cut that had provided the Germans with excellent cover. Trees now surround the area but by the summer of 1916 there was little vegetation left intact. One tree did survive and its grey, sun-bleached trunk and a few wizened, skeletal branches still stand today. This is the Danger Tree, it stands isolated in no-man's-land, a miracle of survival.

We walked through the site and through the trenches and across to Hunters Cemetery and past Y Ravine itself, just a small clough or dell, where red signs warned of unexploded ordnance. A little further on we reached Y Ravine Cemetery.

The Newfoundlanders were not the only Regiment to have fought to capture Beaumont-Hamel; alongside them were the men of the 29th Division. And the 51st Highland Division would also see action here. In Hunters Cemetery 46 of their number are interred. A further 110 lie in Y Ravine Cemetery. The Battle of The Somme cost the 51st Highland Division more than 2500 casualties –wounded, killed or missing. In the spring of 1917 the Germans withdrew eastwards from The Somme, leaving me to think all that loss of life had been for nothing. Y Ravine Cemetery was created in May of that year to rebury the dead that had been interred in temporary graves on the surrounding battlefields.

Since the First World War the poppy has been associated with the British Army. This bright, cheery scarlet flower bloomed every spring and summer in profusion on the devastated battlefields of the Western Front. Men of the French Army chose the blue cornflower as their emblem. For the Newfoundlanders, as I was to discover whilst wandering through the visitor centre at Beaumont-Hamel, the pale blue forget-me-not was symbolic.

We had spent an hour visiting the trenches, shell holes and cemeteries at Beaumont-Hamel and as we returned to the bikes the car park was beginning to fill with cars and coaches. We cycled on, through a verdant landscape of flat agricultural fields and fields thick with poppies that were so unlike the cratered landscape we had so recently left. At the quiet village of Hebuterne five workmen in high vis jackets were mooching about the church yard, all seemingly unwilling to start mowing the grass. Of more interest was a plaque on the outside wall of the church yard commemorating the Bradford Pals. We cycled close to Gommecourt Wood, scene of such terrible loss of life for the Sherwood Foresters. A little further on at Foncquevillers I spotted a plaque to the Staffordshire Regiment, 'one day we will understand' said the inscription. Would we ever understand the futility of war and of this one in particular?

Just before another village we stopped close to a small copse on the edge of agricultural fields. Whilst I crawled into the dense undergrowth snagging my legs on brambles and stepping over nettles for a comfort break that was anything but comfortable Mike consulted the sat nav for our route into Arras. A few minutes later as we were stood astride the bikes having a drink a cyclist approached from the direction of the village.

"Bonjour," he called, cycling across the road and stopping in front of us.

His bike was a high spec carbon fibre affair, gleaming red and white, unlike our aluminium alloy framed road bikes that were by now anything but gleaming. His bike might have been considerably lighter than ours but he certainly wasn't. His racing club lycra hugged his body in distressingly unattractive ways. Lycra can't half stretch. He was obviously fit though despite his rotund tummy, with huge muscly calves and thighs. Assuming we were in need of some directions he began chatting in French and pointing at the map.

"Sorry, Anglais," Mike apologised.

"Ah, oui!" nodded the French cyclist before proceeding to chat optimistically and persistently in French even though it was obvious we were struggling to understand a word he was saying.

For the next five minutes there was a lot of laughter, much chattering in both French and English, quite a bit of shrugging and a lot of gesticulation.

"Arras," Mike said.

"Ah, oui, Arras," nodded the cyclist, pointing up the road, before adding something else we couldn't understand.

Mike added a few sentences of his own, the Frenchman looked perplexed but nodded anyway and then added a few French phrases at which point it was our turn to look perplexed. Then the cyclist spotted my scab covered arm and knee.

"Ouch!" he said sympathetically, proving that there was at least one word common to both languages.

I nodded, said "Ouch!" in reply and mimed falling off my bike. At which point both Mike and the French cyclist rolled their eyes.

"Where?" ventured the Frenchman.

"Zeebrugge," I offered, not entirely sure of the name of the town in which the incident that was to plague me with injury for the rest of the summer had actually occurred.

"Western Front," Mike attempted, waving our guide book.

"Ah, oui! Tres terrible!"

He then mimed that it was going to rain. We nodded sagely. And then, our limited communication skills now exhausted we all put our feet on the pedals and waved each other off with a mix of bye byes and au revoirs.

From there it was just a short ride to Arras and we stopped on the southern outskirts of the city to have lunch on a bench by a small stream. The midday sun was hot and we were grateful of the shade offered by a cherry tree in full blossom as we sat eating bread, crisps and bananas.

"What are you doing?" I asked as Mike began to construct himself a sandwich using all three ingredients.

"Making a cheese and onion crisp and banana sandwich," he replied, like it was the most popular of sandwich fillings. "They're really good, you should try it."

"Hm, I'll stick to eating them all separately thanks."

A white duck dabbled in the stream in front of us, not as brave a couple of mallards that came out to snaffle crumbs from around our feet. Two joggers ran past, looking hot and energetic and scattering the ducks as they went by.

"What time can we check in to our apartment?" Mike asked.

"From four o'clock onwards but we need to contact the owners with a time so they can meet us there," I replied.

"I was wondering if they'd let us arrive sooner, that way we could leave the bikes and explore the town on foot. It might be worth asking."

"Hm, I suppose so." I sent off a quick email to the owner, not really expecting to get a reply, and put my phone in the pocket of my cycling top to make sure I heard it ping if a reply did come back.

Lunch over, we packed up and cycled along a quiet cycle route into Arras and to the Arras War Memorial and Cemetery on the south-western edge of the city. Another designed by Sir Edwin Lutyens and unveiled in July 1932 by Lord Trenchard who had commanded the Royal Flying Corps during the War, the Arras War Memorial consists of a long front wall behind which are colonnaded cloisters, with the graves sited in a grassy open area to the rear. The wall upon which the names of the missing are inscribed, runs for some distance along a busy main road, inside this wall on numerous panels there are almost 35,000 names of British, South African and New Zealand soldiers most of whom died during the Battle of Arras between 9th April and 16th May in 1917 and who have no known grave. Others who died in this area up until the end of August 1918 and whose bodies were never found are also commemorated on the panels here. The graves, arranged in serried rows behind the Memorial wall, number some 2650, with a further 8 graves being added during the Second World War. Of the graves from the First World War, two were executed by firing squad, one for desertion and the other for striking an officer; it seems unbelievable today that such offenses were ever considered to merit such extreme punishment.

During the Battle of Arras the Royal Flying Corp saw heavy action as they fought for control of the sky above the city, their loss was so great that that month became known as 'Bloody April'. Therefore it is fitting that on a square of lawn just inside the entrance to the Arras Memorial sits the 5 metre tall Flying Service Memorial, topped with a globe. The globe was sculptured by Sir William Reid Dick and it is set at the same angle as Earth was at on Armistice Day in 1918. It commemorates the 1000 airmen who died on the Western Front and have no known grave.

At the beginning of the war, with aviation in its infancy, The Royal Flying Corps was small, with just a few personnel and 66 aircraft. But the role of the aviators was to become increasingly vital to the war on both sides, and within two years this number had grown to squadrons, with increasing numbers of pilots and ground support. Their role had widened too to include not just reconnaissance and aerial photography but combat and bombing raids. By the end of the war the Royal Air Force had come into being and aircraft numbered 1800. Safety for the pilots had been slow to improve and to be a pilot or aircrew was still one of the most dangerous of all the services, the planes were unreliable and flimsy and the chances of being shot down were high.

The Royal Flying Corps provided vital air support throughout the Great War and life expectancy of the pilots ran to hours and minutes rather than weeks and months. During the Battle of Arras alone the Corps lost 75 planes, with 19 air crew killed, 73 missing and 13 wounded. The loss of life for soldiers on the ground seems bad enough although around one fifth of these soldiers survived the First World War, by comparison over half of men serving in the air services were injured, killed or missing.

The high walls seemed to block out the traffic noise and the cemetery was a peaceful, sunlit place. We left the bikes outside to walk through the cloisters and the cemetery, reading the inscriptions on the walls and the gravestones. Some relatives visiting the memorial had left photographs of the dead, laminated to protect from the elements, the old sepia prints were often accompanied by a brief biopic or message and fastened next to the name inscribed on the memorial or left on the stone seating that ran around the base of the inscribed wall. Yet again so many lives lost, young men in their teens, twenties, thirties, a few even in their forties.

Birch trees lined the grass in front of the red brick perimeter walls of the cemetery and in front of each headstone shallow flower beds grew peach coloured roses, oxeye daisies and clumps of blue bedding plants. In one corner of the cemetery there stood approximately twenty headstones, identical to all the others but bearing the names of German soldiers. In this war at least, the enemy was no more to blame than our own soldiers; they had all believed they were fighting for king and country. A little further away and I came across another collection of headstones, soldiers of the Indian Army. All the fallen had been given the same honour in death regardless of nationality, race or faith. What a shame that this compassion and respect had not been in evidence in the summer of 1914 when hate, power and megalomania had ruled the crowned heads of Europe, when the honouring of decades-old Treaties had been thought more important than the honouring of human life.

Just as we were returning to our bikes and I had given up hoping the owners of the apartment had read my email, my mobile pinged. It was always pinging! It pinged every time a message came up on messenger (which was quite frequent with the group of eight brilliant but daft friends and colleagues I was in). It pinged when a text came in. It pinged if I forgot to lock the screen before putting it in my pocket (another frequent occurrence which often resulted in one or more of the group messaging to say I was pocket texting again). It pinged when Chris contacted me on WhatsApp. It pinged just now interrupting my train of creative thought (a train that was often slow-moving and frequently managed by Southern Rail). And at two minutes to two on that sunny May afternoon in Arras it pinged to let me know an email from the apartment owner had indeed come through. Yes they could meet us at the apartment in ten minutes. Ten minutes!?

"They will meet us in ten minutes," I read out loud.

"Ten minutes?" gasped Mike.

"Yes ten, rapidly shortening to nine, minutes!"

"Okay, what's the address of the apartment?"

I snatched up my phone and inadvertently turned it off. It pinged considerately to let me know my stupid mistake.

"Sodding hell," I snapped, or words to that effect.

"What?"

"Just switched the phone off," I muttered, fumbling to switch it back on.

The screen swirled and whirled with the colourful opening graphics meanwhile ice caps melted, species became extinct and Trump's supporters came to their senses, actually no, it didn't take that long. Mike meanwhile was consulting his sat nav app and preparing to enter the address of the apartment. Finally my phone's opening graphics finished and I was able to access my email.

"Okay, it's Rue de… er, erm… It might be easier if I just spell it."

"Here, let me see," said Mike, leaning over my shoulder to read the address. He tapped it into his phone.

His sat nav app, whirred and thought and then…

"No! We're not there! Keep up will you!" Mike barked at the phone.

"We've got to be there in six minutes," I said agitatedly.

I don't like being late. I begin to stress even if I'm going to be late for something as trivial as going to the library. Mike ignored me, a sure sign either he was stressed or he was having problems with digital technology, the former usually resulting from the latter where Mike is concerned. A not uncommon condition of the twenty first century, I fear.

"Right, this way!" Mike said, mounting his bike and still clutching the phone in his right hand.

I followed him for all of five feet before he stopped suddenly in front of me.

"What have you stopped for?" I snapped, nearly falling off the bike.

"The red light," he snapped back.

"That's for cars, not us," I snapped right back at him.

He didn't move, dithering about for the green light to appear before setting off into a stream of traffic. I followed a little more cautiously and then found myself having to put a spurt on to catch him up as we got closer to the city centre. The sky was darkening like our mood as the forecast afternoon rain began to threaten. He stopped suddenly again, to consult his phone. I glared at him, he muttered something grumpily and then we set off again. Ah, the joys of a shared cycling holiday. At one point we dismounted, having found ourselves on the wrong side of a busy dual carriageway in the heart of the city and needing to cross to a side turning. Walking the bikes and heaving them onto the curb and pushing them for fifty yards was easier than trying to negotiate the four lanes of traffic and two more sets of traffic lights. The sat nav app was consulted again and again it was clearly found wanting.

"No! We're not there! Keep up will you!"

It's a good job we weren't cycling with a parrot, it would have arrived home from holiday with a colourful if limited range of phrases. I opened the email on my phone and tapped the link to open the map attachment. It opened, the sat nav app on my phone kicked in (not sure how, don't ask, beyond me!) and it suggested we head for six miles in completely the opposite direction to where Mike's phone was suggesting.

"Are we here?" I tentatively asked him, proffering the phone.

"Yes, but the apartment isn't where your phone thinks it is!"

"Okay, I'll ignore it then," I mumbled and returned my phone to my back pocket from whence it issued lots of pings and then a couple of dings. I'd probably just sent my bank details to someone in Nigeria but never mind. We didn't have time to worry about that, we had an apartment to locate.

"This way!" said Mike, quickly getting back on his bike and turning left and then right.

I hastily followed and there around the corner was a tall town house bearing the sign 'Rue de er, erm…' and under the sign was a young woman hovering on the doorstep. Eureka, we had found it!

"Bonjour!" she smiled. "Mrs May?"

Well, not quite but I wasn't going to split hairs at this point, and besides which I didn't know what French for Ms was.

"Hello!" I replied. "I am so sorry we are late, we got lost."

"It is okay you are only five minutes late."

Five minutes? It seemed more like five hours! I was still gabbling apologies and profuse thanks for allowing us to arrive early as she led the way into the building and along a dimly lit corridor. A door on the left opened onto a tiny courtyard where we were to leave our bikes. She waited as we removed the drink bottles and the panniers, just as we were doing so there was a clap of thunder and rain began pouring from the sky in biblical proportions. She thrust a large plastic sheet at Mike, instructing him to cover the bikes, and both she and I dived inside, leaving Mike to struggle on his own with the sheet. Well, no point all of us getting wet, was there?

Dripping and squelching behind us, Mike followed us up a flight of winding stairs to the second floor and the door to our apartment. She gave us a quick guided tour, pointed out the fridge with its bottle of milk and pats of butter, the kettle, the tea bags, the coffee maker and then asked what time we would like breakfast. Having decided on 8 o'clock she then told us she would leave the breakfast basket in the cupboard on the landing. She gave us the code for the wifi and for the combination lock to access the front door, then wished us a pleasant stay and departed, possibly to mop the stairs.

Left alone we explored the apartment. It was clean and minimalist but well stocked with a small kitchen, dining and living area that was divided from the bedroom by a panel wall with windows in the upper half. Two doors which suggested a couple of walk-in wardrobes were actually access to the shower room and the toilet. With the exception of the sink, the toilet and the ceilings which were all white, and the floor which was grey, everything else was black: the walls, the bedding, the curtains, the table, the kitchen work surfaces, the sofa. I went to hang my black waterproof jacket on the hook behind the door and then thought better of it. It blended into the wall and I feared would never be able to find it again.

As Mike slumped soggily onto the black leather settee I put the kettle on and unpacked our own teabags. We watched rain pour down the window and listened to the thunder rumbling overhead as we sipped tea, ate the complimentary biscuits and chocolate caramels and debated what to do next.

"A third cup of tea, I think," I said getting up and going to put the kettle on again.

"Then a quick shower, change into dry clothes," added Mike. "And then we could go out and have a look round the old city. If it stops raining!"

"We can still do that, there's an enormous black umbrella lurking behind the door."

"How did you manage to see that?"

"I didn't. I tripped over it."

Mike rolled his eyes.

By the time we had both showered and changed the rain had stopped and the sky was clearing. We left the apartment, walked a few yards down the street and emerged into one of the main squares. Arras is the capital of the Pas-de-Calais department of France and is a vibrant, busy and at times traffic clogged city. Arras like Ypres was devastated by bombing during the First World War, and also like Ypres it has since been rebuilt to match the original. The gable buildings surrounding the cobbled squares are faithful copies of originals that dated from the seventeenth and eighteenth centuries, many of the premises on the ground floor now home to shops, bistros, cafes, bars and small tourist-centred businesses. There are two large main squares, the Grand Place and the Place de Heroes, the latter renamed following the Second World War and the sacrifices of the local French Resistance fighters. Markets have been held in the squares for the last 1000 years, but unfortunately not on any of the days we found ourselves there. We strolled across the cobbles, where once soldiers would have rested there were now parked cars.

Arras was never in German hands but the German Army had surrounded it on three quarters of its sides. Vitally important, sited as it was on major rail and major road links, the Germans tried many times throughout the war to capture the city. As a result Arras was comprehensively bombed causing vast devastation and the loss of hundreds of civilian lives. The Germans specifically targeted any tall landmarks that the Allies used as observation posts. Famously, the Belfry was shelled numerous times, amounting to significant damage, until it finally succumbed to the sixty-ninth shell and collapsed completely. It had stood as a symbol of hope and freedom and the remaining citizens and the regiments of Allies stationed there took it as a bitter blow. How any citizens managed to survive in the ruins is astonishing, most did so by living a stifling existence in the cellars, coming out to seek food and to socialise with the Allied soldiers stationed there, grateful for their support in the war. By the time the war came to an end three quarters of the city had been destroyed, it became known as one of the Martyred Cities of France.

We crossed the squares, where it was easy to see on some of the buildings the shrapnel marks in the old stones that remained, the new stones standing out with cleaner, sharper lines, and the markings on some of the walls that had been rebuilt using shuttered concrete. The dedication to the faithful rebuilding of such a vast number of buildings across this old city was astonishing. We were heading for the famous belfry, one hundred years ago it had been in ruins, piles of dust covered rubble in the square, now it was as architecturally grand as it had been before the war. We paid the small fee and rode the lift up the tower to emerge on the walk way in front of the bells, we climbed a short spiral staircase, went through a door and came out onto the balcony just below the clock face.

The views from the belfry were stunning. In the distance we could see the site of the battlefields, the ridge at Vimy, fields and woodlands. In the far distance on a hill were the ruins of Mont-Saint-Eloi, an abbey which had been damaged and robbed of much of its stone during the French Revolution, then further damaged during the war and now left in ruins as a monument to the war. Closer to hand were the suburbs of Arras with the many more modern buildings and immediately surrounding the belfry the restored and rebuilt squares, merchants' houses, cathedral and churches. With an audible click the clock hands above us moved to four o'clock and Mike raced inside hoping to see the bells striking the hour. Had it been closer to midnight he might have stood a chance but by the time he had dashed round the tower to the door, gone in and dashed down the stairs the bells had struck four times.

"Too late?" I asked as he emerged panting from the door a minute later.

"Or too early – by about six hours!" he laughed.

Views taken in and photographs taken we returned to the lift and the ground floor where we looked round the information centre. The sun was shining brightly as we strolled across the square, with me pausing every few shops to gawp at all the chocolate displayed in the windows. If Mike was thinking it was taking me a long time to pass some shops he should wait till we reached Bruges.

Next stop for us was the cathedral. From the outside, this building too bore traces of shrapnel damage, original stones that could be saved and left in place had been, but many showed signs of damage. Originally there had been an abbey here, but in 1804 Napoleon gave it an upgrade when he decreed it was a cathedral. Rebuilding had already been taking place after the French Revolution and the new cathedral was rebuilt in Greco Roman style with soaring arched roofs supported on towering pillars, much carving of both wood and stonework, and with a highly ornate interior. In less than a year from the beginning of the war Arras and its scores of bell towers and its grand buildings were in ruins. The cathedral was still standing but it had suffered considerable damage with many of the buttresses, windows, arches and the main doors being destroyed. On 15th July 1915 the Germans targeted the adjoining abbey buildings with fire bombs. The library was ablaze and the fire spread along the roof beams and into the cathedral. Much of the abbey and the cathedral were destroyed, including important ancient documents, but priests and the congregation managed to save many items of religious and historical significance, at great risk to their own lives. The fire was extinguished but the Germans had not finished with the cathedral and over the next few days they continued to target the building until much of it collapsed. After the war, debate raged – should the cathedral be rebuilt and restored? Should Arras be rebuilt in a manner faithful to the pre-war city? In the end, under the direction of architect Pierre Paquet, the cathedral was faithfully rebuilt, wherever possible the same materials were used as the originals, many of the original stones were collected for reuse, traditional craftsmen were employed for the wood and stone carving and for the ironwork. It was a long process and the finished cathedral was finally officially opened in 1934.

The cathedral was quiet and almost empty as we strolled down the aisles, risking neck ache to peer up to the arching roof and the high windows. In one of the side aisles eight panels mapped 2000 years of Christianity; if nothing else it illustrated that war, genocide and famine had been prevalent for the last two millennia, and man has learned nothing from history, except perhaps how to wage war more effectively.

We left the cathedral and stepped into a more modern building looking for something other than history and culture, namely our meal that evening. With the kitchen available to us we decided to break with tradition and shunned the baguettes and cheese for pasta with tomatoes, mushrooms and basil. Traditions are hard to ignore completely, so a couple of delicious looking items from the patisserie counter also found their way into our basket along with beer and chocolate.

We returned to the apartment and were faced with the challenge of the combination code door lock. Not to worry! I had memorised it.

I'd also taken the further precaution of taking a photo of it on my phone but I was confident my brain training was going to pay off. I tapped in the code and pushed the door. It didn't move.

"Are you sure you've remembered it correctly?" asked Mike, beginning to sag under the weight of groceries. It was not an unfair question, I am dreadful with numbers.

"Yep, I'm positive," I asserted. I tapped the code in again. The door still refused to yield.

Mike raised an eyebrow, a nice change from the eye roll I knew and loved. I took my phone out and began scrolling through the photos. Justification at remembering correctly competed with frustration that the door still would not open.

"Perhaps you need to try pushing the door," I suggested. "You're more forceful than me. And heavier." I added.

I entered the code once again and stepped back as Mike threw himself against the door. It was like witnessing a drugs raid. The door flew open and he catapulted into the hallway, disappearing into the gloom with a rattle of beer bottles, a rustle of carrier bag and a startled shriek.

"You better not have squashed those cream cakes!" I said, stepping in behind him and closing the door whilst trying not to laugh.

He hadn't squashed the cream cakes and I didn't manage not to laugh.

A brief hour and a half later, food cooked, meal eaten and washing up done, we were setting off once again to walk to the citadel.

"Should we take the umbrella?" asked Mike.

"Not sure I can find it again," I answered.

"It's supposed to rain again soon," he cautioned. "We might not get as far as the citadel."

We set off optimistically but sat nav and building black clouds soon got the better of us and we returned just an hour later, without reaching the citadel and just as the first heavy drops of rain began to fall. Within minutes the lightning and thunder began. Rivers of water washed down the streets, bouncing off the roofs, overflowing gutters and choking downspouts with the volume of rain. We stood in the bedroom windows, watching the storm as we had three nights previously in another bedroom on the other side of the city. My phone was pinging merrily as the girls on messenger began commenting on the storm back at home. It seemed as if half of northern Europe was experiencing a storm that evening.

"The power's just gone," pinged in Charlotte.

"Ours went half an hour ago," pinged Mary Anne.

"It's woken Jude and I've spent the last half hour trying to get him to sleep!" pinged Claire.

"I hope my house doesn't get struck again like last year," pinged Crystal.

"Our power's gone now," pinged Alison. "I can't see to open the Prosecco."

"I thought you could do that blindfolded!" we all pinged simultaneously.

"Workplace bullying!" pinged Alison in rely.

The thunder storm carried on far longer than the pinging, and we went to bed that night to the sound of thunder claps and rain drumming on the windows.

Friday 1st June 2018. 57 miles.

Mike's socks that morning matched his handle bar tape, although they would have matched several colours of bar tape. For reasons best known to a man not renowned for his sartorial elegance he had brought his pair of supermarket Christmas socks. If pulled up to their full extent they revealed a Christmas elf wearing a green, red and blue stripy outfit. Why had I not noticed earlier in the week?

"You can just fold those socks down before you step outside with me this morning," I commented.

"What's wrong with them?" he asked. "You bought them!"

"Hm, they were a stocking filler. They seemed like a good idea at the time. I never envisaged cycling through France with you wearing them!"

We left Arras in busy morning rush hour traffic, cycling out to the citadel that we had not been able to reach the evening before. We crossed the bridge over the moat where coots and moor hens swam in the reedy fringes and over the bumpy cobbles, through a large arched gatehouse and into the vast walled compound. Buildings that had once been barracks and headquarters now seemed to house offices, and conference rooms. In the far corner of the parade ground a group of teenage students were being put through an exercise drill.

We left Arras along a convoluted route through the northern suburbs that inevitably included a couple of wrong turns before we were out into the open countryside and the quiet villages once more, following lanes that ran between fields of corn. Everything seemed to be going well, progress was being made and then the sat nav, which Mike had set to bicycle mode, suddenly decided to take us on a route that even tractors and quad bikes would have struggled with. We retraced our route for a short while then followed an alternative main road option until we were able to get back on track. Trucks and cars whizzed down the road, passing close to our panniers and stirring up dust as they rushed by. It was a relief to turn off onto a quieter road and before too long we reached a familiar landmark. It was the German Military Cemetery at Neuville-St.-Vaast.

This was the one we had cycled past on our way from Vimy Ridge earlier in the week, now we were approaching it from the front. The German cemeteries were somewhat different and this one in particular was a far more humble affair than the British, Commonwealth and French cemeteries. Austere as you would expect but functional too. Why should the enemy be given more than brief deference by a country ravaged by invasion? And so for many years following the end of the war, recovered German dead had often been interred in mass graves, whilst the already existing German cemeteries that had been created by the Germans during the war had been left and the graves neglected for many years. The German cemeteries that we did come across bore rows of simple crosses, although other German cemeteries did have ornate grave stones and monuments. By the end of the war there were sixty eight German cemeteries along the Western Front but over the years these have been consolidated, often with the soldiers' remains being reinterred in Germany. Today there are four German First World War Military Cemeteries along the Western Front in

Belgium and four on the Front in France, each contain the remains of over 125,000 and 89,900 soldiers respectively.

The simple metal crosses embossed with the name, dates and regiment of the soldier were set in neat rows amongst the grass. The only break in these lines of matching crosses were a few traditional thin stone headstones; these marked the graves of German Jewish soldiers and bore the Star of David carved at the top of the headstone. Some 100,000 Jews served in the Germany Army during the First World War, of these 12,000 died for their country. Less than a generation later and their country seemed to forget their sacrifice. Trees dotted the graveyard but there were no flowerbeds and no big ostentatious monuments. We walked through part of the site, scattering fallen leaves with our feet. The Cemetery is the largest German Military Cemetery of the First World War to be located in France, and holds the remains of nearly 45,000 German soldiers, most died in the fighting in the area of Artois, Lorette and Vimy Ridge over a three year period from 1914 to Easter 1917. The French military authority had established the cemetery in the five years after the Armistice, bringing remains of German soldiers from around the region to this one final resting place.

We continued on the straight road that climbed steadily uphill. The views were opening out across this once war-ravaged landscape and in the distance on our right we could see the Canadian Monument at Vimy Ridge. At the top of the rise there were two cemeteries facing one another across the road. On the right, a Polish Cemetery, and on the left one containing members of the Czechoslovakian Army. In contrast to the simple German Cemetery at Neuville-St.-Vaast, the Czechoslovakian one had an ornately carved memorial stone at the entrance. It was easy to forget how many different countries in Europe were dragged into this far-reaching bloody conflict.

Cresting the brow of the hill we enjoyed the descent to a cross roads where we diverted left to the French and British Cemetery of La Targette. On the right hand side of the site stood the familiar rows of British headstones, with their neat flower beds in front of the rows; on the left of the site the much larger area containing the simple crosses of the French graves stretched into the distance, a vast number. There are 599 British graves but 11,443 French ones, with a further 3282 unidentified French soldiers' remains in an ossuary. Most of those who lie here died at the Battle of Artois.

Back on the main road it was no time at all before we arrived at the British Cemetery of Cabaret-Rouge. Here the headstones were arranged in concentric circles around the central altar, found in nearly every British Military Cemetery of the First World War. Neatly pruned shrubs formed an open circle around this central table and beyond this on the far back of the graveyard stood the memorial cross, another constant in all First World War British Military Cemeteries. Larger trees were dotted around the cemetery and at the end of each row of headstones grew purple flowering lavender. This cemetery with its less than standard layout had been designed by Brigadier Sir Frank Higginson. He had worked for the Imperial War Graves Commission for nearly forty years and died in 1958. To honour his wish, his ashes had been scattered in this cemetery. His wife died four years later and her ashes were also scattered here. They are in good company, over 7500 British, Canadian, Australian, Irish, Indian, South African and New Zealand soldiers and airmen are interred here. A large proportion, over half of these, are unidentified. This is partly because the cemetery was an 'open cemetery' taking the remains of the dead as they were discovered, often many years after the end of the war.

Next followed miles of quiet roads passing through villages where there seemed to be few inhabitants and little traffic. So when a car did appear coming towards us, a bright pink Fiat 500, I quickly spotted the driver waving from his open window and grinning at us. He looked different in a car instead of in Lycra but it was the friendly cyclist from the day before. I barely had time to register the fact and grin back before we had passed one another.

Cycle paths along the pavement kept us off the road through one village where a small boy walked along carrying a baguette as big as himself. The roadside verges were full of wildflowers, brightly coloured with camomile, poppies and dandelions.

Navigating our route through Loos-en-Gohelle proved challenging. The sat nav was taking us on a course that resembled one of those maze puzzles in childhood comic books. Mike was getting frustrated and I was too as we found ourselves cycling through a less than salubrious neighbourhood of social housing, where dogs barked manically from untidy front gardens that reminded me of the grimmer parts of my home town. At a bend in one residential street the sat nav suggested we go straight on and then bear slightly left. Straight on was up a grassy bank onto a former inclined rail track that had once served the coalmines of the area. After some consultation we wheeled the bikes up a faintly worn footpath through the grass and onto the top of the incline. Wheeling the heavy bikes down the other side proved more challenging as I struggled to control the descent with my incapacitated shoulder. The pedal smacked into the back of my right calf, tearing the skin.

"What have you done now?" asked Mike, seeing me rubbing my leg.

"Whacked the pedal!" I exclaimed, dabbing at the trickle of blood.

"You're going to be one big scar by the time we get home!" he sighed sympathetically.

I am never surprised by my hopeless mispronunciations of French words. But on learning the correct pronunciation for Loos was 'Loss' I was struck by the tragic irony of it. For losses there were here on a tremendous scale, at least 45,000 soldiers from both sides died in just six weeks.

The Battle of Loos occurred in autumn of 1915, and was part of the larger offensive of Artois-Loos. The terrain was challenging, the troops were tired from previous fighting and there was a shortage of shells. But the number of British troops far exceeded the number of German and it was thought the Allies had a good chance of achieving their objectives. Four days of intensive shelling by the British Army preceded the start of the battle but it had not been enough and the British used poison gas for the first time. The wind changed direction, blowing the chlorine gas back over the British lines. Panicking, blinded in their ineffectual masks and choking on the burning acid forming in their lungs the British soldiers lost seven men and 2600 were wounded.

The Germans had used poison gas effectively for the first time in April 1915 at Ypres. At the time the only protection available to Allied soldiers was to urinate on a cloth and hold the sodden material up to the nose and mouth. Having condemned this gas attack as an atrocity the British quickly went on to develop their own poison gas. It triggered a race by both sides to produce more deadly effective chemical weapons. Urine soaked handkerchiefs were hurriedly replaced by basic respirators that looked little more effective and soldiers were issued with goggles, later full face gas masks were introduced although some soldiers hated to wear these uncomfortable and suffocating masks and in the panic of a gas attack many struggled to put them on in time. Those caught in a gas attack were severely injured if not killed. Chlorine gas reacted with moisture in the lungs creating hydrochloric acid, anyone who inhaled the gas effectively suffocated as the lung tissue swelled. The later use of mustard gas caused even more horrific injuries. It was a vesicant that not only killed by inhalation and suffocation but burnt both the skin and the airways, burning through uniforms and causing suppurating blisters on the skin and blinding anyone without eye protection.

Meanwhile at the Battle of Loos things were progressing far more successfully to the south with mainly Scottish Divisions capturing Loos and Hill 70. But this was short-lived. Armaments were running low, reinforcements were running late and the Germans retook Hill 70. The next few weeks were a familiar story of gains and losses, with many occurring at the infamous Hohenzollern Redoubt, a strongly defended and fortified section of the German line. On 13th October another attack on the Redoubt was attempted, gas was deployed again by the British Army and the 46th Division advanced. Within ten minutes they had lost over 3700 men. In total the British Army suffered 20,000 dead at Loos, with a further 30,000 injured. Owing to the type of fighting in the area most of these dead were not recovered until after the war. By this time the remains were impossible to identify, and many of the graves in the cemeteries around Loos are inscribed with the words 'a soldier of the Great War'.

Rudyard Kipling had been a resolute supporter of the Great War with his vitriolic writings against Germany and his unfaltering belief in Britain's part in the war; he was a leading public figure at the time. When his teenage son, John, was initially turned down by the army due to poor eye sight, Rudyard Kipling used all his influence to have John accepted into the Army. Kipling's persistence paid off, or not as the case may be, and John was enlisted in the 2nd Battalion of the Irish Guards; he arrived in France on the day of his eighteenth birthday in 1915. In less than two months, on 27th September, Lieutenant John Kipling went over the top leading his men in the Battle of Loos. Heading towards Chalk Pit Wood they had an area of open ground to cross, an area of land on which the Germans had trained their machine guns. The battle was a disaster. John Kipling's body was not found. Rudyard Kipling poured his grief into attempting to discover what had happened to his son. He hoped he had been captured and, using his contacts in neutral Sweden, attempted to find out if John had been taken prisoner by the Germans.

Kipling died in 1936, bitterly changed by the war and the loss of his adored son, and never knowing the final resting place of John. But in St Mary's Advanced Dressing Station Cemetery in Haisnes a few miles to the north of Loos-en-Gohelle the grave of a soldier 'Known unto God' was to have its inscription changed in 1992. The confusion over the identity of the dead soldier came about as John was known to have been promoted just before he went missing, the uniform this unknown soldier had been wearing was of the wrong rank. However, it was later to be believed that there had been insufficient time to update the uniform following the promotion, and additionally all other dead lieutenants in that area on that day had been identified and accounted for. The Commonwealth War Graves Commission changed the headstone and finally 77 years after John Kipling died he was no longer solely 'known unto God'.

The headstones are in their own way beautiful, the cemeteries too are beautiful. And it is thanks to the work of Rudyard Kipling and Winston Churchill that the headstones and their arrangement in the cemeteries are not influenced by rank, regiment or social standing. They are all equal in death, whether identified or known unto God.

We eventually escaped Loos. Not before passing another cemetery in the midst of another residential area and close to a small industrial estate. Then in the late morning we came to yet another cemetery, this one containing the graves of Portuguese soldiers. The arched entrance gateway was ornate with numerous carvings and topped with a stone cross.

We were now on the cycle path at the side of a wide main road, in the distance we could see a busy crossroads and to the left of this was located Neuve Chapelle Cemetery. We often hear of the Canadians, Australians and New Zealanders and the sacrifice the men of those nations made for the Commonwealth but lesser well known is the number of Indians (men from the now partitioned India, Pakistan and Bangladesh) who fought for Britain in the First World War. At the outbreak of the war the British Army brought the many military units already in existence from the Indian subcontinent to the Western Front. They came from hot countries to Northern Europe, to cold, rain, mud and they suffered dreadfully. Neuve Chapelle Military Cemetery is, for many, their final resting place. The monument lists their sacrifice: 4857 missing in action, 206 prisoners who died in German prisoner of war camps. More than 400 of them died at the Battle of Neuve Chapelle alone where the Indian regiments made up half the numbers of those fighting. So it is appropriate that the monument, designed by Sir Herbert Baker (who also designed Tyne Cot Cemetery) should bear the Star of India and a lotus flower and be flanked by two stone tigers. The design is based on the idea of an Indian sanctuary with a nod to Indian shrines, and the column bearing the Star of India was inspired by those built throughout India in the 3rd century BC by Emperor Ashoka. Appropriately there are inscriptions in not only English but three languages of the Indian subcontinent

India did not just supply soldiers to fight for Britain during the war; 50,000 Indian labourers worked behind the front lines to resupply troops, dig trenches and dozens of other tasks that were often dangerous, dirty and tiring. By the end of the war 140,000 men from across pre-partition India as well as Burma and Nepal had served the British Army either as fighting troops or labourers; of these 50,000 were injured and 8600 were killed. And India was not the only country supplying labourers, thousands of Chinese men toiled building railways, roads and trenches, and moving supplies and armaments for the Allied war effort.

The sunny morning had turned into an overcast midday and we had just cycled into another small town, where a quiet main street was lined with trees and flower beds, when there was a sudden and torrential cloud burst. We leapt off the bikes, taking shelter under one of the trees but the downpour was too heavy and the tree too small to be effective and we hastily riffled through our panniers for our waterproof jackets. A passing van driver tooted to gain our attention, shouting out of the window and pointing further down the street. He was directing us to a bus shelter but Mike had already spotted a shop awning immediately across the street and we darted across for the better shelter it offered. A passing shop keeper seemed to suggest we could wait in her premises even though everywhere seemed to be closed for lunch, but I was unsure if that's what she was really implying and she had hurried out of sight before we could follow.

We passed the time as the rain poured down, missing our heads and bodies but splashing our feet, and had some lunch while we waited for the shower to ease. I had all kinds of bits of nibbles stashed away in one of my panniers and out came biscuits, half a bar of chocolate, a rather bashed banana, an apple and a squashed packet of sweet chilli flavour crisps.

After half an hour the shower was becoming lighter and we decided to carry on. We left the small soggy town along a quiet country lane awash with standing water and muddy puddles. A large modern tractor overtook us, forcing an oncoming car off the road and nearly into a deep drainage ditch. The driver looked irate as his vehicle teetered on the edge of the verge. The tractor was pulling a trailer filled with onions and the smell as it rumbled past was strong enough to make your eyes water. I noticed the ditch on the right seemed to be full of onions. Had the same farmer tried a similar manoeuvre before with less success?

Suddenly there was a three way junction on a quiet road, an old building with faded whitewashed advertising on the side, and the metalled road surface ended to be replaced with cobbles. This was the Belgian border but there were no official signs to indicate this, just the change in road signage style and language and the sudden appearance of dedicated cycle tracks.

We joined a wide concrete cycle track parallel to the main road and screened by a row of trees, and continued heading towards Ypres. The architecture was subtly changing too, all the houses now seemed to be of red or yellow brick with pale mortar. The land was rising as we drew near to Kemmelberg. With its views across to the ridges at Messines, Wijtschate and Ypres Kemmelberg had been strategically important and had remained in Allied hands since the beginning of the war. But in the spring of 1918, when increasing numbers of American troops began landing at the coast, the Germans decided they needed to make another bid to capture the ports, in order to do so they had to break through the British front lines that ran along these ridges to the west. Having pushed through the Allied front line at Armentieres to the south, the Germans attacked Kemmelberg on 25th April 1918. Fierce fighting with heavy bombardments and much use of gas on both sides continued until 10th May when the Germans captured Kemmelberg. By then the once pleasantly wooded hill with its carpets of wildflowers was a crated, muddy morass with twisted, fractured trees scattered across the hillsides and pockets of gas still lingering. French forces to the north managed to halt any further German advance, but in the Battle for Kemmelberg over 5000 French soldiers lost their lives.

We cycled through the cobbled streets of Kemmel and out up the increasingly steep road, at 17% it was the steepest of the holiday, to the mass grave where the French soldiers were buried. At the time of the end of the battle it had not been possible to gather the dead, and it was not until the spring of 1919 when their remains were finally laid to rest in the mass grave. By then there was little to identify many of the soldiers, and of the 5294 that lie there only 57 could be identified. We had become accustomed to seeing high proportions of headstones in many of the Allied military cemeteries bearing the inscription 'known unto God' or 'a soldier of the Great War' but not to this extent. The French grave was surrounded on three sides by a low stone wall, neatly mown grass covered the site together with a few trees. In the centre was a stone obelisk and at the rear the French flag flapped in the breeze. Further up the hill and looking down onto the cemetery from the top of the hill stands a carved angel atop a 60 feet high column.

Nearby are the Lettenberg bunkers, and leaving the bikes propped against a fence post we walked along the leaf strewn path between the trees to reach them. The bunkers and a network of tunnels that run under the hillside behind them were dug by the British at the beginning of the war and were used for communication and shelter and were a vital observation post. The Germans captured them in spring 1918 and used one as a first aid post. Access to the tunnels has been sealed but it is still possible to go into the bunkers, ducking under the low corrugated concrete roof, but it is harder to imagine the life endured by the soldiers who were stationed here during those terrible years. Today one of the bunkers is sealed off to protect the long eared bats that now inhabit it.

We enjoyed the lazy descent on quiet roads devoid of traffic, racing down the lane between stands of trees, until we reached another remnant of war but this one dating from a much later period. Cordoned off behind a wire fence and set back in the trees was a bunker built during the Cold War. What would the 5000 French dead a little further up the hill have made of the political turmoil that continued to dog the twentieth century, I wonder?

It was not far to Ypres and we reached the outskirts as the Friday afternoon rush hour began. Avoiding the traffic-clogged centre we turned off on a quieter lane that curved around the old city walls, following the moat. The route was not without its hazards though and Mike was nearly knocked off his bike as a woman driving a black BMW reversed erratically out of a parking space whilst looking the other way. It was only Mike's quick reaction that prevented an accident; the woman drove off oblivious to the near miss.

As I knocked on the door at the same Bed and Breakfast we had stayed at a week earlier the door was opened immediately by the owner. He must have been standing right behind it.

"Julia! You're back!" he cried bouncing out of the door. "Have you had a good trip?"

"Yes thanks," I replied.

"And you too?" he asked turning to Mike. "I forget your name," he added almost dismissively.

"Mike. Yes, thanks."

We removed the panniers, stowed the bikes, helmets and gloves in the garage and followed the owner into the house. He had given us the same room on the ground floor which meant we could immediately relax in the loungers on the terrace whilst enjoying the complementary beer and tea. Mike passed the biscuits as I slumped back in the lounger. I was struggling to sit up without sliding down the lounger, the lycra cycling gear I was wearing seemed to be excessively slippery on the nylon fabric.

"What are you doing?" Mike asked as I floundered about.

"Can't stay upright!" I gasped sliding down and nearly spilling my tea.

"I know that!" he replied, rolling his eyes. "That's been your problem since de Haan!"

"Shut up and pass me the biscuits please!"

He did, reaching across as I slumped even further down the lounger.

"What is that smell?" I asked wrinkling my nose.

"Oh, I think it's my gloves."

"You're not wearing your gloves."

"I know, but they've got a bit skanky and the smell seems to linger on my hands. I need to soak them in disinfectant."

"I'd do your gloves as well, if I were you," I commented wryly.

"I meant my gloves!" And then as the penny dropped, "oh, very funny."

Eventually, replete with tea and biscuits, Mike helped me out of the lounger and we went to have a much needed shower before walking back into the centre of Ypres for an evening meal. Even though we were an hour earlier this time, the square in front of the Cloth Hall was as busy as ever, the pavement cafes were full and the supermarket even busier than the previous time we had been there. We bought supplies for our by now standard picnic tea but there had been a run or possibly a plague of locusts on the patisserie section, and there was little left to choose from. Out of desperation – not greed, you understand – we were forced to buy of box of four cream cakes. The baguettes, cheese and salad we ate sitting on a bench in the square, the cream cakes had the potential to be a little messy and so we decided to save them for later. Crowds were already making their way to the Menin Gate even though there was more than an hour before the ceremony began. We were both quite tired and as the evening was quite cold we decided not to wait for the ceremony and made our way back to the B&B. It was as well we did. As we entered the drive we could see there were two more guests already there and busy preparing to make use of some of the owner's bikes which he allowed his guests to borrow.

"Hi there," said the young woman, introducing herself and her husband.

They were intending to cycle out to a nearby New Zealand cemetery that evening.

"This is the only opportunity we will have," explained her husband. "We're catching a train to Paris in the morning."

Mike's bike was already sitting on the drive and the husband went back into the garage and brought mine out. I assumed he had to move them both in order to reach the owner's folding bikes but I had assumed wrong and so, as it turned out, had he. As his wife stood there on the drive, wearing a helmet identical to Mike's, I suddenly realised they were about to cycle off on our bikes. Mike obviously reached the same conclusion at the same time.

"Er, those are actually our bikes," he remarked.

"Oh my god, no! I'm so sorry!" exclaimed the woman turning red with embarrassment. "And I'm wearing your cycle helmet too!"

"It's okay," we reassured them.

"We thought they were rather good quality to be lending out to just anyone," her husband said. "Sorry about that. We'll take these folding ones, they'll just be a bit slower."

We left them replacing our bikes and went into the house.

"I notice she'd not put your gloves on!" I laughed.

"It's a good job we came back when we did," Mike said thoughtfully. "If they'd had a puncture or something it would have set us back tomorrow morning."

We took the box of cakes into the kitchen where I cut each one in half and made another cup of tea while Mike searched through the kitchen drawers for a bottle opener. Cakes cut, beer opened and tea brewed we went back outside to the sun loungers on our little private patio. The cakes seemed a lot smaller now they were cut in half.

"Last patisserie of the holiday," Mike commented wistfully.

"No, we'll get some more tomorrow to eat on the ferry," I replied. In the end we didn't, so I feel even less guilty about us eating four in one sitting.

Saturday 2nd June 2018. 61 miles.

We thought we were having an early breakfast at 7 a.m. but the New Zealanders had already eaten theirs and were preparing to leave as we entered the kitchen that morning. They apologised yet again for the mix up with the bikes and then had to explain to the curious owner what had occurred.

"Never mind, at least we didn't get back to find our bikes missing!" I reassured them.

"So, you're getting the train to Paris this morning?" asked Mike.

"Well, we were, but they aren't running now. There's a strike on!" replied the young man.

"Another?"

"Yes, the French are always striking," declared the Belgian B&B owner. "I will take these young people to the bus stop and then return in ten minutes."

He left us fending for ourselves with cereal, yoghurt, toast and a swarm of house flies that were causing as much irritation as the French rail workers. He returned ten minutes later and settled down at the breakfast table to begin a diatribe on the French workers which quickly turned into a racist rant about migrants, asylum seekers and finally drug addicts and benefit scroungers. After fifteen minutes this turned to the European Union, Brexit and border control and before we knew it we were back to asylum seekers.

We finally escaped to our room where we packed up the panniers, filled the water bottles and changed into our cycling gear. Ten minutes later and we were off on the final leg of our bike ride. It was approximately 60 miles that day to return to Zeebrugge via a different route than our journey south. The day was much colder and for most of it we were cycling in long sleeved tops. We headed eastwards to Sanctuary Wood and Polygon Wood but we were not alone on the roads that Saturday morning, there were lots of club cyclists out, whizzing along on an array of carbon fibre bikes, clad in matching club colours and overtaking us at regular intervals.

Sanctuary Wood is approached down a quiet lane and is now home to a small museum with a preserved system of British trenches. The farmer who owned the land here returned after the war and decided to preserve the trenches and the shell holes so that today it remains as one of the best examples of original British trenches on the Western Front. The trenches, lined with corrugated metal supported by wooden uprights, zigzag through the wood. They are not quite as deep as the German ones at Bayernwald, in fact in comparison to the German ones the Allied trenches were inferior in many ways. They were invariably muddy, sometimes with timber or sandbags shoring up the walls, and often with earth sides that were prone to collapse in wet weather and thus made 'going over the top' an even greater hazard. German soldiers were able to walk through their trenches which were lined with planks of wood instead of ploughing through mud, and stood dry footed on even floors. For the German Army trench foot was far less of a problem than the Allies. Walls of the German trenches were also stoutly shored up with wooden planking and overall had better protection both from the physical conditions and from enemy shelling.

It is preserved trenches like these which give an insight into the conditions of the First World War as little else can. Old, jerky black and white footage or stills of the Western Front invariably depict the mud, the miles of trenches, the duck boards, skeletal trees, shell holes flooded with rainwater, soldiers climbing the ladders and going over the top to be cut down by the scything crossfire of bullets, rotting corpses of men and horses half submerged in mud. It is a grim reality that today's green Flanders fields show little evidence of. The horses that did not rot where they fell were swept into huge graves, the soldiers whose bodies were recovered were given their own individual plots in the numerous cemeteries. Much of the building materials used to construct fortifications were recycled and reused by returning civilians, just as Britons plundered Hadrian's Wall for building stone after the Romans left Britain. Some of the trenches survive, well preserved monuments in their own right and a history lesson suspended in time. There are memorial bunkers such as those at Hill 60 on the Ypres Salient. A few of the pill boxes also remain, such as the German ones near Messines and at Tyne Cot, and these now act as monuments to battle. The contradiction of a German pillbox, sitting on Belgium soil, commemorating New Zealand soldiers is a strange one that today warrants little consideration, but at the time the Kiwis were falling in their thousands it would surely have seemed absurd.

Sanctuary Wood and the Hooge sector of which the wood forms a part saw heavy fighting for much of the war. Within less than a year of the outbreak of the war the village of Hooge was little more than a pile of ruins and the German Army frequently targeted the area. In June 1915, following the erection of further German strongholds, tunnels were dug by the 175th Tunnelling Company and the largest mine of the war to that point was detonated under the German bunkers in the evening of 19th July. The Middlesex Regiment and the Gordon Highlanders advanced before the stunned Germans had time to recover, the resulting mine crater was taken and the British front line advanced. Within the month the Germans retaliated, using flame throwers for the first time with devastating effect.

From Sanctuary Wood we turned in a more northerly direction heading to another wood that had been the scene of fierce fighting: Polygon Wood. The current woodland here covers a much smaller area than that covered before the First World War. In the midst of this, set back from the road rises a manmade hillock that had been created by the German Army and into which they had excavated a series of bunkers. Like so many other places this area of land changed hands several times during the war. In September 1915 the 5th Australian Division captured the wood. Their sacrifice is commemorated by the memorial that now sits atop the hill overlooking New Buttes British Cemetery where over 2100 Commonwealth soldiers were laid to rest, more than three quarters are unidentified. Close by is the New Zealand Memorial which commemorates officers from that country who died in the vicinity between the autumn of 1917 and spring of 1918 and whose remains were never found. As we stood atop the mound reading the inscriptions we could see a group of Australians wandering around the headstones in the cemetery, one group out of many we had seen at various cemeteries and battle sites throughout that week.

We cycled on, reaching the edge of the wood but had to stop. I had drunk several cups of tea at breakfast and was in need of another comfort break. Leaving Mike holding up my bike, I forced my way into a thicket, ducking down as a large tractor rumbled past. But I ducked a little too far and sat on a nettle.

"Ouch!" I blurted just as a cyclist rode past.

"What have you done this time?" Mike called.

"Nettle!" It needed no further explanation.

"Do you want me to find you a dock leaf?" he joked.

"No thanks!"

Suffering a different kind of saddle sore from the usual, we cycled on following quiet lanes to Zonnebeke and the largest British military cemetery on the Western Front: Tyne Cot. Just when I was beginning to think I could no longer be struck by the same sense of despondency and futility at yet another monument, yet another cemetery, yet another stretching line, row on row of grave stones representing yet more lost and wasted lives I would see another symbol of the Great War dead and feel the same emotions over again. By now we had seen so many cemeteries and memorials, but how had it come about that all along the Western Front, across Belgium and down through France, areas of land had been set aside for Commonwealth military cemeteries?

After the Great War the nations of France and Belgium gifted parcels of land for the creation of military cemeteries and gave permission for the building of memorials. 2316 military and 2000 civilian cemeteries in France and Belgium hold the graves of over 725,000 British and Commonwealth dead. Over fifty countries sent men to fight on the Western Front, many had never left their own local area before and many would never return. As the war raged many of the dead were never recovered, their bodies blown to pieces, vaporised, buried by explosions or rotting where they fell, further destroyed by more shelling until the boys and men they had been were unidentifiable, unformed, little more than fertiliser for future generations of Flanders farmers. Of the remains that were recovered many were buried ad hoc, some to be exhumed by further bombing, some to later be recovered and reburied in a Herculean task that was undertaken by the Imperial War Graves Commission established in 1917. This would later become the Commonwealth War Graves Commission. Inevitably many graves were never recorded or the records were lost but by the end of the war the IWGC were aware of the location of some 150,000 graves strewn across the Western Front. Many of these, it was decided, would be moved to what became known as concentration cemeteries. These cemeteries line the Front, strung out at depressingly regular intervals. By 1921 there were 132 completed cemeteries in France and Belgium. The design of the cemeteries is quite standardized, something the IWGC was keen to establish from the start. Each gravestone is made of Portland limestone, and is carved with the casualty's name, rank, unit, date of death, age, and either a national emblem or regimental badge and the appropriate religious symbol. At the time the family of the deceased were permitted to add a short personal dedication, at a cost of three and a half pence per letter, it was only later that this fee was made voluntary. We were to see few gravestones that indeed bore these personal epitaphs. Refreshingly, for a conflict that had seen Generals and high ranking officers safe, warm and well-fed far from the immediate dangers of the front, in the cemeteries no consideration was given to rank, and Privates rest in peace next to generals, equal in death even if they had not been in life. Architecturally the cemeteries are also standardised. Low walls or neat hedges border the graveyards. Each cemetery has a metal cupboard containing a Cemetery Register. Depending on the size of the cemetery there will be a Cross of Sacrifice or a Stone of Remembrance. Thought was also given to plants, trees and shrubs within the cemeteries in the hope of giving an air of English country garden to these places where so many hundreds of thousands of British and Commonwealth soldiers were laid to rest. Today all this uniformity and order gives an impression of peace and respect, but at the time when the cemeteries were being laid out and when the British Government had expressly refused to repatriate any of the dead this authoritarian treatment of the fallen was detested by many grieving relatives. Some even went so far as to attempt to exhume the bodies of their loved ones. But the British Government and the IWGC maintained their policies and today, unlike public cemeteries where the wealth of the dead is reflected in the elaborate memorials, in these First World War cemeteries the war dead are remembered for their sacrifice rather than their wealth and social standing.

One hundred years after the end of the First World War bodies are still being recovered along the Western Front and many archaeological digs have taken place along the Front in recent years. A group of amateur archaeologists called The Diggers have, between 1992 and 2000, excavated the remains of 155 soldiers at Boezinge near Ypres. Many of these soldiers had died where they had fallen between the trenches and received no formal burial. Among their remains personal items were often found: bibles, diaries, combs, mirrors. I recall watching one television programme covering one archaeological dig that uncovered several soldiers' remains, on one the archaeologists found a mirror. Tarnished but still functional the archaeologist remarked that he was the first person to look in this mirror since its owner had been killed. It was a poignant and personal reminder of the human side to the First World War. And no doubt if the gift shop in Albert could get their hands on it they would be selling it on!

As the largest British military cemetery in the world it was no surprise to find Tyne Cot was served by a visitor centre and a large car park with a small block of toilets. Even though it was quite early in the morning we were not the first to arrive, a couple of cars were already parked up and a large coach followed us into the car park. The cemetery is enclosed by a large stone wall behind which stands a colonnaded walkway engraved with the names of 35,000 missing soldiers, mainly British and New Zealanders. The curving lines of headstones mark the graves of 12,000 soldiers, less than 4000 of these are identified. Some of the headstones list the names of three or four men buried together, one headstone simply reads 'Eight soldiers of the Great War'. The dead here at Tyne Cot lost their lives in the years of heavy fighting around Ypres, but most died during the Third Battle of Ypres, which came to be known after the village around which much of the fighting took place, the emotively named Passchendaele. Tyne Cot is sited on what had once been a German stronghold and one of the blockhouses that had once been a German Advanced Dressing Station, now forms the base of the memorial Cross of Sacrifice at the centre of the cemetery. A gap in the limestone blocks reveal the original concrete wall of the German bunker beneath, and wreaths of poppies stand against the monument. The remains of two further pillboxes are situated towards the bottom of the cemetery.

Mid-morning and we cycled into the village of Passchendaele, just the sound of it is emotive and the events that were to unfold here in the summer of 1917 secured this once quiet Belgian village a bloody place in history. At the time of the Battle of Arras in spring 1917 the true objective for the British Army was to break the German hold of ports on the North Sea at Zeebrugge and Ostend, ports that were being used as U-boat bases. The first part of this plan was to attack the Messines Ridge, part of the Ypres Salient. The attack was carefully planned and relied heavily on tunnels running deep into the earth and far under the German lines into which mines were placed. On 7th June, following 5 days of artillery bombardment, the mines were detonated. 450 tonnes of high explosive ripped up through the German front line, the sound carrying as far as the south coast of England. It was a success for the British Army and after just four days of fighting both the German front line and its reserve line had been captured.

Continuing the plan the next attack came at Passchendaele, the Third Battle of Ypres on 31st July 1917. Two weeks of artillery bombardment had already been taking place but on the evening of 31st July it began to rain. It was the worst summer rain in forty years. Craters and shell holes filled with water and mud. Any drains that had been put in place had been destroyed during the bombardment. The sun never broke through for long enough to even begin to dry out the ground. Into this swamp of mud and blood soldiers on both sides fought, fell, died and rotted away. Typical of many of the battles of the Great War, Passchendaele dragged on, through the autumn months and into November until the village of Passchendaele was finally captured by Canadian soldiers. The Third Battle of Ypres had come at a heavy cost, over a quarter of a million German soldiers had died, and the Allies lost over 325,000 men.

We cycled through the village of Passchendaele and down the long straight street to the Canada Gate. This arched metal gateway is one of a pair, symbolising the steps taken by the Canadian soldiers on their journey from their homeland to Passchendaele. The first gate stands in Halifax, Nova Scotia where 350,000 Canadians, including native peoples and immigrants, embarked on the ships that would bring them to the Western Front. This second Portal of Remembrance marks the place where to quote the memorial 'for thousands, their last steps in life were taken here'. Passchendaele was to become the worst fight in the military history of Canada, 4000 men died and 12,000 were wounded. But the Canada Corps fought on for ten days, during that time they advanced just 700 metres but it was enough to capture Passchendaele which they did on 10th November 1917.

In April 1918 the Germans struck back, hoping to gain ground before the arrival of reinforcing troops from the U.S.A. and so they began the Lys Offensive. It took the German forces a mere three days to push the Allies back to Ypres. All the land gained at such a high cost in the Third Battle of Ypres was lost.

From Passchendaele we followed quiet country lanes, lined with apple orchards, vending machines selling strawberries, fields of potatoes and cabbages. Crows strode between the rows of vegetables searching for insects and worms. At Westrozebeke we joined the former railway line, one used by the German Army to supply the front line. It was a lovely path to cycle along, slightly elevated for much of the way above the surrounding fields and popular that Saturday morning with local cyclists. At Staden work was taking place on a new memorial and the cycle path looped round the site of the works, it was possible to see where the original rails had been left in situ. This was a flat landscape once more, the cycle route was lined with poplars providing shade as the morning became increasingly hot.

We left the railway route, joining a main road but once more the cycle route was on a separated track parallel to the road making the journey far more pleasant. Woodland lined one side of the road for a while, interspersed by farmland and housing. It was a dead straight road through a flat landscape, not the most inspiring of cycle routes and as lunch time rolled around we began to look out for somewhere to buy some food. Eventually we saw a familiar blue and yellow sign in the distance and pulled in to the car park of a German discount supermarket. The debate began – should we buy food for our evening meal too or should we wait until we reached Zeebrugge? To carry or to risk finding a supermarket nearer to the port? Remembering the Hook of Holland and its well supplied small retail complex we decided to just buy enough for lunch. We must stop doing that! We opted for some sliced pepperoni, a baguette and a punnet of fresh strawberries, then set off looking for somewhere suitable to sit to have lunch. It wasn't long before we found a shady seat in a small woodland on the edge of the road. It wasn't long before every blood-sucking insect in the wood found us. With half the strawberries left untouched we found ourselves hastily packing up and setting off once more.

This part of Belgium had been spared most of the fighting and destruction of the First World War. The Germans had swept through here at the beginning of the war, capturing the ports and pressing on to the west only to be halted in their advance by a tactical manoeuvre that stopped them in their tracks and held their advance in this part of Belgium for the entire war. The Yser front in the northern part of Belgium was a natural barrier to the German's advance, here the inundations of the Yser river posed difficulties to the Germans. This area from Nieuwpoort on the coast south to beyond Merkem is predominantly flat and at high tide is actually below sea level. The land here is drained extensively through a network of ditches and canals, and the navigable part of the river Yser is controlled by locks at Nieuwpoort, which we had cycled past at the beginning of our holiday. At the beginning of the war the German's Schlieffen Plan was to advance through here and capture Paris. In a bid to stop this the Belgian Army formed a front line some 22 miles to the west of the Yser Canal. But the Battle of Yser saw the Germans advance, crossing the river. The situation looked grim until a local superintendent of the Northern Waterways, Karel Cogge, suggested the sluice gates at Nieuwpoort be opened to flood the area. His plan was approved and in October 1914 the gates were opened. The resulting marshes were over a mile wide and stretched as far south as Diksmuide. The German's 'Race to the Sea' to gain control of the ports of Dunkerque and Calais and their planned advance on Paris was over. Karel Cogge's bright idea was rewarded by a knighthood.

Cogge's idea meant that throughout the war Germany only had access to a limited number of ports, and as the bitter war dragged on through four long years the German civilian population slowly began to starve. In April 1917 the U.S.A. finally joined the war. Their entry gave the Allies hope but still the war dragged on. By 1918 this war of attrition was still one of advance and retreat all along the Western Front. Under Hindenburg and Ludendorff the German Army launched a spring offensive hoping to break the by now much weakened French and British Armies, this was the so-called Kaiserschlacht (the Emporer's Battle). The German Army made colossal advances, driving the British back to the Somme and even launching artillery fire onto Paris. But in order to maintain their advance the German Army needed to restock and resupply, artillery needed to move forward and the muddy roads, churned up by heavy artillery bombardment, once again proved an obstacle to the horse drawn heavy guns and supplies. Operation Michael, part of the German Army's plan to split the French and British Armies and hasten an end to the war, was called off. Thousands of lives were lost on both sides for no significant gain.

At the end of March Operation Georgette was launched with the Germans attacking near Arras and Amiens, then in early April they attacked on a smaller scale near Ypres. The spring of that year saw Germany attack along various points on the Western Front with mixed success. But despite many setbacks and retreats for the Allies, the British industrial might meant the Allies were able to replace lost and damaged armaments. Germany ultimately could not keep up with this arms race and Ludendorff was beginning to despair. On 8th August the British Army attacked at Amiens, forcing the German Army back eight miles. With better strategic planning and use of the R.A.F. to provide support for advancing soldiers and tanks, the British Army drove the Germans back. By the end of

October the Austro-Hungarian Armies had been defeated in Italy, freeing up more Allied troops to reinforce those already on the Western Front. The Allies realised that if they continued a series of offensives along the Front they stood a chance of defeating the Germans that year. Ludendorff was ready to seek an Armistice by late summer but he found the terms offered unacceptable. He later resigned his command. Eventually, on 3rd November, the Germans requested an Armistice. Kaiser Wilhelm abdicated on 9th November. Germany had succumbed. The Armistice came into effect at 11 o'clock in the morning on 11th November.

The war was finally over. Somewhere in the region of a million British men were dead. Virtually every town and village in Britain had lost men, only a few communities were spared, these are the Thankful Villages. There are none in Scotland and Ireland, and just 53 in England and Wales. In France, where even more men enlisted to serve in the First World War, there is just one Thankful Village, Thierville in Upper Normandy.

The serving soldiers did not immediately get to return home, there was work still to be done among the devastated landscape, such as locating bodies for burial, decommissioning weapons, packing up and clearing away. The horses and mules did not get to go home at all. After all they had been through their fate was to go to the butchers of a hungry France. On being demobilised each soldier received his back pay, a rail warrant and, for some, a gratuity based on rank and length of service. Needless to say an officer's gratuity was more than that given to a private. Generals received the largest of all. Haig, questionable leader and commander in chief, did rather better than most, receiving an Earldom, a nice statue in his honour which stands in Whitehall, and a very generous lump sum of £100,000. That's £1 for every British and Commonwealth soldier killed. He apparently accepted this amount reluctantly, not out of humility you understand, oh no, it was half what he had originally asked for.

At the time, the Great War was described as a war to end all wars. It was not. It never will be. French General Foch famously said of the Treaty of Versailles "This is not a peace. It is an Armistice for twenty years."

We reached the ancient city of Bruges in the early afternoon. We crossed a couple of busy roads where coaches were idling as they dropped off hordes of tourists, and followed a lane into the cobbled heart of the old centre. Bicycles and people were everywhere. So were horse drawn carriages and people balancing precariously on segues as they enjoyed some of the more exciting options for exploring the city. The bumpy cobbles were excitement enough for me and fearing either a wheel jamming in the gaps or someone stepping into my path without looking, both potentially ending with me coming off again, I decided to push the bike.

All the streets were lined with tall brick buildings, on the ground floor nearly all were given over to shop premises, upper floors seemed to be a mix of offices, hotels and apartments. Most of the shops were either trendy boutiques or chocolate emporiums, and the smell wafting out of many doorways was intoxicating. The prices of the chocolates on display were a little less dreamy.

"Ten Euros for a tiny box of five chocolates!" I exclaimed after browsing in one shop.

"What do you want any more for? We got a bar of chocolate at Lidl," Mike replied.

"It's hardly... Oh never mind!"

Once, thousands of years ago, Bruges had been on the coast but tidal deposits had extended the coastline away from the city. There had been Bronze and later Iron Age settlements in the area and later the Romans arrived, fortifying the city to guard against pirates. By the ninth and tenth centuries the area had become permanently settled and by the early twelfth century Bruges had been granted its city charter and this marked a period of expansion as new walls and canals were built, increasing the city's security and its ability to trade. With its position close to the coast and on a crossroads of important trade routes, by the Middle Ages the city was thriving, and Bruges was once one of the world's major commercial cities. Of particular importance was the wool and cloth trade. But by the 1500s the Zwin Channel, Bruges' access to the coast, and known as the Golden Channel for the wealth it helped to create, was beginning to silt up; other North Sea ports such as Antwerp were taking over the bulk of the trade. In the seventeenth century lace making was important to the city but the golden era was over and Bruges dwindled in importance. It was not until the era of tourism in the latter half of the nineteenth century that the city began to grow once more.

Bruges was occupied by the Germans from the beginning of the First World War, it fell peacefully to their advance and as a result Bruges was left virtually undamaged. It was finally liberated in October 1918. Fast forward to 1940 and the German Army was back but again Bruges got through the war virtually unscathed. To survive two world wars and retain nearly all the original buildings is a rarity for most European cities whose countries were involved in the conflicts. So it was unsurprising to discover that Bruges is a UNESCO World Heritage Site. Today visitors of all nationalities visit Bruges, and tourism, chocolate, diamonds and lace seem to be the life blood of the city. There is, apparently, a chocolate museum.

How did we miss that? But if horror and ghoulish interests are more your thing there is the Torture Museum. Or for a bit of the religious macabre there is always the Basilica of the Holy Blood, which supposedly houses a relic of Jesus' blood collected by Joseph of Arimathea after the crucifixion.

The large central Markt Square is surrounded by grandly gabled buildings, with innumerable small windows and intricately carved stonework. There is a fourteenth century City Hall occupying one side of the square. A thirteenth century belfry stands out above the other buildings with its 83 metre high tower. It was easy to see why tourists came in their thousands every year to visit this beautiful little city. From one of the buildings a clock was chiming two as we wheeled our bikes into the middle of the square. Flags flew in front of many of the buildings, grand statues overlooked the pavement cafes and old fashioned lamp posts were dotted across the square. Ranks of bicycles were parked up, pigeons swooped in to peck food from under peoples' feet, a balloon modeller entertained the crowds in one corner of the square and a line of horses waited patiently in harness for their owners to drum up business for their tours of the city. Everywhere there were people like us, cameras in hand, trying to get photographs of the beautiful square and its old buildings without getting someone's head appearing in the shot. A group of cyclists entered the square just as we were leaving it.

"Hm, the smell of horse muck and chocolate!" I heard one of them say in a broad Yorkshire accent.

After consulting his sat nav, we left the centre of Bruges on what Mike had been expecting to be a scenic route along a canal. If your interests run to recycling stations, scrap yards and industrial warehouses then you would no doubt have enjoyed the next few miles of cycling. Those highlights were on the left, on the right was a narrow ditch fringed with reeds, although this did widen after a while to be tempting enough for a family of ducks to show an interest. The canal on the left came into view beyond the last of the warehouses, a wide commercial body of water, it is still used to freight goods into Bruges from the coast and is lined by a series of wind turbines. The highlight of that 'scenic' bit of cycling was watching a cormorant on the canal. After a few miles of this scenic bliss we reached a road crossing the canal and we crossed too, to follow the cycle path along the other bank of this broad body of water. We were nearing the coast now and nearing our boarding time and I was beginning to worry that we would be cutting it fine if we were to also find a supermarket. After a couple of miles of cycling along with trees on one side and water on the other, and seeing hardly any other people we came to a junction where a lane came in to join the towpath from the left. At this point we needed to carry on along the towpath which would take us to the coast at Zeebrugge. There was just one problem. It came in the form of a little, fat man in a high visibility vest and baseball cap.

"Closed," he said. "Cycle race."

To emphasise his point a small peloton of amateur cyclists whizzed round the corner at that point and sped off along the towpath. There had been no indication when we joined the towpath that it would be closed further on. Could we just continue and keep to one side?

"Closed."

Could we perhaps wheel the bikes carefully along the road to reach the main road?

"Closed."

Could he see we were now in a quandary as we tried to find an alternative route to the coast? Of course he could, he was watching us with a mix of curiosity and disdain. I was beginning to think we were going to miss the ferry. And I was thinking of the many times on my cycling holidays where I had got lost or been faced with diversions and road closures, and there had always been someone stepping forward helpfully to offer directions and advice. The man in Holland with his bag of croissants. The Swiss couple who told us to follow them as they led us through a village on the Rhine. The taxi driver in Galashields who pointed me to the B&B. The couple from Bolton who took pity on a cold, soggy cyclist in Scotland and fed me tea and biscuits in the back of their car. I had encountered so many helpful, pleasant individuals over the years. Unfortunately the fat, little, high vis, baseball capped Belgian wasn't one of them.

"Closed."

"Is there an alternative route we can take?"

"No. Closed."

Furious at his lack of help or concern and by now becoming very anxious that the time wasted retracing the last two miles and then having to find an alternative route could mean we would miss the ferry, I am ashamed to say I lost my temper.

"Thanks, you've been a big help!" I said sarcastically.

"You're welcome. You're a nice lady," he replied equally sarcastically.

"No, I'm a pissed off lady!" I snapped, turning my bike and cycling furiously back the way we had come.

Mike followed, making no attempt to keep up, as I set a blistering pace back down the towpath. Eventually I ran out of steam and stopped to wait for Mike. We then began our own race to the sea as we spent a frustrating hour route finding as we tried to avoid a busy trunk road which we were unsure cyclists were even allowed on, and even if they were it was not the sort of road we would choose to cycle down as it was full of juggernauts travelling at speed towards the port. They too had a ferry to catch. Eventually, after following a dusty farm road for several miles we reached a main road with a cycle track alongside. The cranes at the port of Zeebrugge slowly drew nearer as we cycled flat out for the coast. It had been a fraught hour, hot and dusty and tiring.

Zeebrugge is not like the Hook of Holland. There is no significant centre and there were no significant shops. The town seems to be a concrete mass of roads and buildings strung out along the coast; hot, dusty, sandy and unappealing. We found a French supermarket that was super low on stock and super high on prices and instead of the tempting salads we had contemplated buying in Lidl earlier in the day, found our selection limited to some sad looking bread rolls, crisps, a packet of lambs lettuce and tomatoes. Wishing we had bought the salads when we had the chance we grabbed a few items and began looking for some patisserie to soften the disappointment. There were none. Maybe a beer? Mike wasn't impressed by the selection so we ended up with a carton of fresh orange juice instead. Not quite what he had in mind but at least it was healthy.

We crammed everything into the panniers, hopped on the bikes and rushed off to the port, only to find that boarding did not close at five o'clock as I had thought but at half past. My panic and our rushing had been somewhat unnecessary. Mike rolled his eyes. We boarded the ferry, securing our bikes to the bulkheads before any vehicles were allowed to board. Preferential treatment? Yes, but the downside was the vehicles would be allowed off first at Hull.

Having found our cabin and luxuriated in long, if somewhat cramped, showers we slumped on the bed. A sign on the tiny dressing table wished us a pleasant voyage and informed us only food purchased on board could be eaten in the public areas. This meant the only place we could eat our meal was in the cabin, and with no chairs and not much room we were forced to eat sitting on the lower bunk, a towel spread over our knees to catch any crumbs. The recent purchases had faired okay but the strawberries had not travelled well. Their juice dripped from our fingers and onto the towel. To add to the mess I spilt orange juice when the ship lurched just as I was opening the carton.

"The crew are going to wonder what I've been doing to this towel," I remarked.

"For goodness sake don't get any chocolate on it!" Mike commented with a grin.

Epilogue

So our cycle ride of Flanders and The Somme was over, we had our own tickets for Blighty and were on our way home. But what became of our relatives during the First World War?

Interestingly, during the researching of family history and military records I discovered, much to my surprise, that my grandfather Herbert Ruddeforth, the sweet faced 16 year old in the old newspaper photograph, had also served in the war. My mum had never mentioned it, and so I had assumed he had never enlisted. But he had turned 18 in January 1918 and with ten months of the war remaining had become a private in the Army Service Corps. His military number was prefixed with the letter M, indicating he had served in mechanical transport. He obviously survived the war, but his life was plagued with breathing difficulties which leads me to wonder if he was ever subjected to a gas attack. In 1922 he married Jane Moore, and in 1932 their only child, Rose was born. I remember him vaguely as a loving elderly gentleman, sitting in front of the coal fire with me on his knee, and later in bed in a downstairs room, in what would have been the parlour in that old terraced house in Burnley, an oxygen cylinder and a mask by his bedside. He died in 1973 when I was five years old.

My paternal grandfather, Frank May, had also served in the war. With the help of his younger daughter, my Auntie Francis, I had learned that he had served as a Private in the Labour Corps. This Corps was founded in 1917 and their work involved the hard physical graft of logistics, rail, road and trench construction amongst other duties. He too survived, returned to Burnley, married and had six children. He died in the late 1960s. I barely remember him.

And what happened to my maternal grandfather's four Ruddeforth siblings, looking young and smart in their Army uniforms in the newspaper cutting from 1916?

Ephraim was twenty when war was declared. He left his job as a weaver in one of the many cotton mills in Burnley and joined the East Lancashire Regiment, Z Company, part of the Accrington Pals, where he served as a Private. He fought on The Somme and survived the war.

Thomas William also joined the Burnley Pals at the outbreak of the war when he was twenty-seven years old. By the time the article appeared in the Burnley Express he had reached the rank of Lance Corporal. He was deployed to Egypt in early 1916. The troop ship transporting the Pals narrowly missed being torpedoed. He was injured in the head and neck by shrapnel whilst fighting in the Dardanelles, but recovered sufficiently to be returned to his unit. The Burnley Pals were then redirected to France ready to take part in the Battle of the Somme. He survived the war.

Willie was twenty-four at the beginning of the war. He was a reservist in the Royal Engineers, serving as a Driver. He survived the war.

Albert, just 19 years old when war broke out, became a Private in the 9th Scottish Rifles. He appeared again in the Burnley Express in August 1916. He had been wounded in the left arm which had been broken, and had been taken prisoner. From my research it appears likely this occurred at the Battle of Delville Wood, part of The Somme offensive. He too survived the war.

It seems nothing short of miraculous that all the Ruddeforth brothers survived the First World War, returning home to the grimy streets, the belching chimneys and industrious factories and mills of this Lancashire cotton town.

William Whalley, my mum's uncle by marriage, was born in Burnley in the 1890s. Before the war he was employed as a carter, and therefore accustomed to working with horses he was enlisted in the Royal Field Artillery as a Driver. Each heavy field gun was pulled by a team of six horses, harnessed in pairs, each pair of horses had a driver, who would sit astride one of the horses. I know he loved animals, I cannot begin to imagine how he must have felt to see the equine carnage of the war. In common with my mother's other uncles, William also survived the war. But not unscathed. He was gassed during one of the many gas attacks, although I have been unable to establish during which battle this occurred. Of all the relatives that served in the First World War, it is William that I know most about, for it was he that mum talked of so much. He returned to Burnley where he married my grandmother's sister Rose Moore. I am named, not after my mum, but after her beloved aunt. As a girl she had spent much of her free time with her auntie and uncle, feeding hens and ducks on their allotment, picking vegetables. He was her favourite uncle, and she his only niece. Childless, the couple doted on my mum and she on them. William died in 1944.

And what of Mike's great cousin John Withers, the farm labourer from Cumberland? Did he too return to his home? Not to the industrial mill town like my forefathers but to the familiar peace and clean air of the Lakeland fells, the mountains, the tranquil lakes, the Herdwick sheep, back to his job on the farm?

... As the ceremony at Menin Gate ended and people began to drift away we climbed the path up onto the top of the grassy rampart leading to one of the outside walls of the monument. We had not consulted the register we were just wandering, reading, looking at the endless carved names and regiments. We were prepared to take our time, and then suddenly, as the echoing sound of the bagpipes dwindled away and the light was beginning to fade Mike called to me.

"I've found him."

One amongst 54,000. It was all there had ever been to find. He died on 3rd March 1916, aged just twenty-one. It seems likely that he was killed during an attack on The Bluff, a mound near the village of St Eloi located to the south east of Ypres. His remains lie in some corner of a foreign field.

The Soldier by Rupert Brooke

If I should die, think only this of me:
That there's some corner of a foreign field
That is forever England. There shall be in that rich earth a richer
dust concealed.....

Facts & Figures

Civilian deaths in the First World War reached nearly 7 million.

65 million men fought in the First World War.

Approximately 2 million German soldiers were killed.

Over 4 million none-white men served in First World War.

Over 5 million British soldiers served on the Western Front. Of these:

In the British Army (which includes soldiers from Commonwealth Countries) the number of men killed was 956,000. And of these over 700,000 were British.

Two and a half million British men were wounded. Of these wounds:

60,000 eyes were lost.

Over 40,000 arms and legs were lost.

By the time the Second World War broke out there were still 600,000 men claiming disability pensions as a result of the First World War.

10% of U.K. men aged between 18 and 25 were killed during the First World War.

The Third Battle of Ypres (Passchendaele) claimed the lives of over half a million soldiers. Of these 325,000 were Allied troops, and 260,000 were German.

An estimated 750,000 soldiers died in the Ypres Salient.

Of these more than 400,000 were either British or Commonwealth soldiers.

Nearly 205,000 men from Commonwealth countries died fighting for Britain during the First World War, almost half of them have no known grave. Their bodies were either never found or, if they were, could not be identified.

Figures from March 2009 from the Commonwealth War Graves Commission show 587,989 men buried in named graves. There are 526,816 listed on memorials to the missing; of these 187,861 were buried but not identified; which leaves 338,955 who could not be buried because their remains had not been found.

7 million rounds were fired by the Royal Artillery on The Somme between 2nd July and 15th September 1916.

At the Battle of Neuve Chapelle 1915 during a 35 minute bombardment more shells were fired than had been used in the entire Boer War.

1.5 billion shells were fired on the Western Front during the war.

The Battle of Verdun lasted for ten months. During that time over a quarter of a million men from both sides were killed. Neither side gained any advantage.

The First World War lasted for four years and three months. During that time over 10 million men from both sides were killed. Neither side gained any advantage.

Author's Note

As I have already stated this is not intended to be a history book. However, inevitably I cannot write about our cycle ride along the Western Front without including much of the history of the First World War. From the start there was a dilemma for me: should I write chronologically about the War or write chronologically about our cycle ride? During the fifty two months of the First World War, battles were fought and refought over the same ground, the same patches of muddy earth on the Western Front; bodies, bloated corpses, rotting flesh and skeletons unearthed and reburied many times by the seemingly endless bombardment and rupturing of the land.

I have chosen to write chronologically of our cycle ride for the purposes of geographical clarity. Within the narrative I have included the history of the battles at the places as we reached them. In some places, such as Ypres, there have been more than one battle over the course of the Great War, and therefore in the narrative there are sometimes descriptions and accounts of battles that have occurred there over a period of several months or divided by months or years. It would be another book to write of all the Battles on the Western Front and of the history of the First World War and I am certainly not qualified for the task.

I hope I have succeeded in giving a flavour of the battles without over-confusing the history of the War, whilst continuing to provide some clarity of the geography and time line of our cycle ride. I have endeavoured to ensure the facts and figures quoted are accurate, and as ever have done painstaking research to avoid any errors. If any errors exist they are mine and they are unintentional. I hope I have given a flavour of the present day sites of the Western Front we travelled through and that I have also done justice to the horrors experienced, and the bravery and the spirit demonstrated, by the men who left their homes and families to fight, and in many cases die, in unimaginable conditions for a cause that few understood.

Find me on Facebook:

For information on charity donations from the sale of 'Cycling Through a Foreign Field' or if you would like to see the photo montage of my forefathers or more photos from this book, or information about any of my books you can visit my Facebook page:

Julia R May Books on Kindle & Kobo

https://www.facebook.com/JuliaRMayBooksOnKindle?ref_type=bookmark

If you like what I do – let people know. If you don't – shh! ☺

Acknowledgements

As ever my thanks must go to a number of people.

My mum, keeper of the carved wooden box. I promise to treasure it and all the memories.

My Aunt, Francis Singleton, for her help with tracing the family history.

Christopher Withers for sharing his memories of his family history.

And of course my partner Mike: lovely, reliable and always ready with an eye roll and a first aid kit. He puts up with a lot.

By the Same Author:

Cycling Across England
© Julia R May 2012
https://tinyurl.com/yc62pful

Two women, two bikes, no backup on a Sea to Sea adventure.

At the beginning of the twenty-first century two friends set off to cycle from coast to coast across England. For one, it was to be the first of many long distance cycle rides.

Cycling Across England is an account of the fun, the food, the mountains, the moorlands and the mathematics the two friends encountered along the way. From the Irish Sea, through the mountains of Cumbria and the Pennine uplands they travelled through a landscape of contrasts to finish their journey in the industrial northeast on the North Sea coast. Broken glass, slugs and arduous ascents were relieved by blackberries, an excess of pizza and delightful descents. Join them as they cycle across England on this iconic ride.

I've Cycled Through There
© Julia R May 2012
https://tinyurl.com/ybxf3gfj

That strangest of traveller, the lone female, is at it again. This time cycling through the heart of England from Bath to London to her home in Lancashire. For such a small country England was proving to be a land of contrasts and surprises; from the leafy lanes of Berkshire to the bleak moorlands of the north, spectacular scenery and post-industrial mill towns, dead divas and murderous mad men.

Throughout the six hundred mile cycle ride there was much that was quintessentially English: Georgian architecture and thatched cottages, William Shakespeare and Samuel Johnson, Bath buns and Yorkshire pudding, canals and Roman roads, Magna Carta and the Houses of Parliament, oh, and Maharajah's Wells and teams of huskies!

Share the experience, the food, the fun and the frustrations. Funny and factual by turns, this is a true account of a cycle journey home through the heart of England.

Walking with Hadrian
© Julia R May 2012
https://tinyurl.com/y9929ggz

A walk through time and fog along Hadrian's Wall.

Built almost two thousand years ago on the orders of the Emperor Hadrian and marking the northern-most boundary of the Roman Empire, Hadrian's Wall is one of Britain's most enduring ancient monuments and a UNESCO World Heritage Site. In 2003 a footpath following the line of the Wall was designated as a National Trail running 84 miles across England from the Solway Firth to the North Sea. Since then walkers have been coming to enjoy this long distance path in the wild landscape of northern England, and a few years later inadvertently choosing the foggiest week she could, Julia finally got round to walking the Wall.

Factual and funny by turns, 'Walking with Hadrian' is an accurate account of the history, culture, scenery and wildlife of Hadrian's Wall Path. Battling fog, maps, social networking and the encroaching perils of middle age, the author has added another book to her collection of traveller's tales.

Cycles and Sandcastles
© Julia R May 2013
https://tinyurl.com/yba8rbqz

Running two hundred miles from Newcastle to Edinburgh, the Coast and Castles Cycle Route promised to be a journey through millennia of turbulent history and fabulous scenery. It proved to be more than just ruined castles and wild coastline. More industrial heritage, more rain, more cross dressing stag nights, more stunning beaches, more wildlife, more grave robbers, more railways, more tea rooms and the Moorfoot Hills.

Close encounters with seagulls, precocious children, warrior-like toddlers and bathroom cleaning products were all in a day's cycling for the author as she pedalled north, passing remote beaches, wooded river valleys and more castles than you could shake a bicycle pump at.

Written with self-deprecating humour and a wry eye for detail, Cycles and Sandcastles is a narrative of the history, the scenery and the flavours of a bike ride through Northumberland and the Scottish Borders.

A Week in Provence
© Julia R May 2014

A much needed autumn break walking in the Verdon Gorge region of Provence turns into a fraught lesson in how not to speak French as the author gets to grips with the language of love, romance and strange combinations of Cs, Qs, apostrophes and genders. Written with her by now trademark self-deprecating humour, this, the author's tenth travelogue, recounts the beauty, the peace and the quieter way of life to be found walking in idyllic rural France.

Never a successful student of languages, but believing you ought to try, Julia displays an enthusiastic if dreadful grasp (or should that be stranglehold?) of the French language as the week unfolds. Whilst coping with a lack of underpants, some rather smelly food and the intricacies of French, A Week in Provence tells of the walks walked, the food eaten, the language butchered and the stretched patience of her long suffering partner as they embark on a walking holiday in south east France.

Bicycles, Boats and Bagpipes
© Julia R May 2014

Having cycled the length and breadth of the British mainland, it was time for a change. After seeing a little blue cycle route sign on the west coast of Scotland, Julia was struck with inspiration. The islands of the Outer Hebrides beckoned. There was just one problem, her boyfriend wanted to go too! Looking on the bright side he could be responsible for navigating and could take most of the luggage. Well, that was the plan. Little did she realise that with her boyfriend there also came his smelly footwear and holey cycling leggings.

Bicycles, Boats and Bagpipes is a detailed and often amusing account of a 500 mile cycle journey through the beautiful and remote islands of the Outer Hebrides and along the mountainous northwest coast of the Scottish mainland.

But it wasn't all about the cycling; there were the rare flower-rich machairs of the Western Isles, idyllic white sandy beaches, blue seas, wild moorland and ancient historic sites to explore. Wildlife to watch. Ferries to sail. Cake to eat and tea to drink. And throughout the trip the experience of isolated communities going about their daily lives, such a contrast from the hustle and bustle of home.

Bicycles, Beer and Black Forest Gateau
© Julia R May 2016
https://tinyurl.com/yctr5bbg

Not many people would consider cycling hundreds miles through Europe to be a relaxing holiday. Mike certainly didn't. But Julia did, she was peculiar that way. There was a challenge to be had in following the River Rhine from its source high in the Swiss Alps, through Germany, France and the Netherlands to the North Sea. But if Mike could not be convinced by mention of the varied scenery, the cultural diversity and the cake, what would change his mind? Finally it was mention of the hundreds of breweries in Germany that convinced him. Who knew, it might turn out to be very relaxing after all?

But as the couple were to discover, cycling on the continent can be very different to cycling in Britain. It was not just the language that would prove difficult to get to grips with, the rules of the road, the navigation, the continental heat and the alpine thunderstorms would test their patience as would tractor drivers and mosquitoes. But most challenging of all would be two weeks without a proper cup of tea. Would beer, gateaux and chocolate be enough to compensate?

Dawdling Through The Dales
© Julia R May 2018
https://tinyurl.com/y8kew292

The Dales Way long distance footpath runs for over eighty miles from Ilkley to Bowness-on-Windermere, encompassing the beautiful scenery of North Yorkshire and Cumbria and two National Parks. It is a varied walk of ever-changing scenery of lush river valleys, limestone pavements, moorland and mountains, and one undertaken by thousands of walkers every year.

When two friends decided to walk the Dales Way over a series of weekends they expected to complete it within a year, but life got in the way. For one of them, the Dales Way would remain an uncompleted long distance footpath.

With details of the scenery, the natural history and anecdotes about the walk, this book will give you a true flavour of walking this often overlooked yet delightful footpath. Light hearted but also darker at times, Dawdling through the Dales, like all of Julia's books, will make you laugh, but it might also make you cry. It is a true tale of walking, divorce, betrayal, depression and enduring friendship.

By the same author but written under her previous name:

My Feet and Other Animals
© Julia R Merrifield 2003

When two friends planned a long distance walk on England's South West Coast Path they thought the toughest challenge would be the walking itself. But the biggest obstacles to be overcome were not the 630 miles of footpaths, or the soaring ascents and descents of the cliffs. They were the unforeseen factors that cannot be planned for but which transform a journey into an adventure. Factors such as a torn calf muscle, recalcitrant underwear, two days of torrential rain and gales, two weeks of the hottest July temperatures for years, high tech equipment designed to help but determined to hinder, the capriciousness of public transport and a host of B&Bs all competing for the title of Worst Accommodation in the West.

Walking Pembrokeshire with a Fruitcake
© **Julia R Merrifield 2004**

Two friends deliberated where to choose for their next walking holiday. How about somewhere different? How about somewhere exotic? How about somewhere foreign? How about Wales? But with countless people advising them where to walk that summer and with neither of them speaking a word of Welsh, had they made the right decision? On a hot August day they set off to walk the 180 miles of the Pembrokeshire Coast Path, starting from somewhere unpronounceable and finishing at a little place called Amroth, passing on the way lots more places they would struggle to enunciate.

Wales, a proud land with a proud past; a land steeped in history, a land of myths and magic, castles and cromlechs, dragons and double consonants, male voice choirs and Aled Jones. Follow their adventures as they search for ice cream vans and a Welsh dictionary.

Pedals, Panniers and Punctures
© **Julia R Merrifield 2005**

One woman, one bike, no backup and 1477 miles on a unique End to End adventure.

Since when did cycle touring become an extreme sport? Since it involved travelling by train. When one woman, more accustomed to long distance footpaths than long distance cycle rides, set out to cycle from Land's End to John o'Groats the first obstacle she faced was getting to the start. Between the start of her journey and the finish, 1477 miles later, she encountered not only ups and downs of terrain but mental and physical highs and lows as well.

Cycling the End to End is so much more than just sitting on something no bigger than, and as hard as, the sole plate of an iron and pedalling, as Julia was to discover. Every experience seemed to be about extremes: Cornish hills, Cheshire plains, busy Devon lanes, empty highland roads, downpours, droughts, smooth cycle tracks, hazardous cattle grids, psychedelic B&Bs and homely hostels. And when the terrain and the weather weren't against her the wildlife was: terrorising Labradors, formation herding sheep dogs, kamikaze squirrels, plagues of midges and road-senseless sheep.

With no backup, and just a bike and a puncture repair kit for company, that strangest of traveller, the lone female, set off to tackle the ultimate British cycle ride. If only she had got a pound for every time someone told her it was all downhill the other way she could have bought a lot more chocolate. As it was, sustained by copious quantities of tea and as much chocolate as she could carry she finally reached her wet and windswept goal.

Walking with Offa
© Julia R Merrifield 2006
Ever heard of a bloke called Offa? King of Mercia, he instigated the building of a defensive dyke. Twelve centuries later a long distance

path was laid out, roughly following the line of Offa's Dyke, and thirty years later still two friends set out to walk it.

How difficult could it be, walking from one end of Wales to the other? Loaded down with maps, guide books and global positioning systems they were soon to find out and only five minutes after leaving Chepstow were monumentally lost! Soon they were enjoying the scenery, watching the wildlife and overdosing on dried apricots. Staying in haunted English castles and heavenly Welsh guest houses they made their way north.

32916397R00097

Printed in Great Britain
by Amazon